3 1368 00068 3874

Y0-BBD-972

EGELSTON JUL 1 2 1972

72-01762

```
Y        Sullivan, George
796.357      Pitchers and pitching
     Dodd     c1972
```

WEEDED

MUSKEGON COUNTY LIBRARY

PITCHERS AND PITCHING

Some major leaguers say that pitching is 75 per cent of baseball; others say it is 90 per cent. Whatever the figure, it is very high.

This book explains and analyzes the art and craft of pitching in detail. Different types of pitches, grips and deliveries, pitching strategy, the subject of control, how the ball curves — all are explored in depth.

How pitchers keep in condition, the duties of pitching coaches, relief pitching, and the role played by catchers are outlined. Final chapters explain how to figure statistics important to pitching, such as won-lost percentages and earned-run averages. Great days in pitching are recalled and baseball's greatest pitchers, as selected by the Baseball Writers Association of America, are profiled.

Nearly 100 photographs and diagrams illustrate the text. All-time pitching records are included.

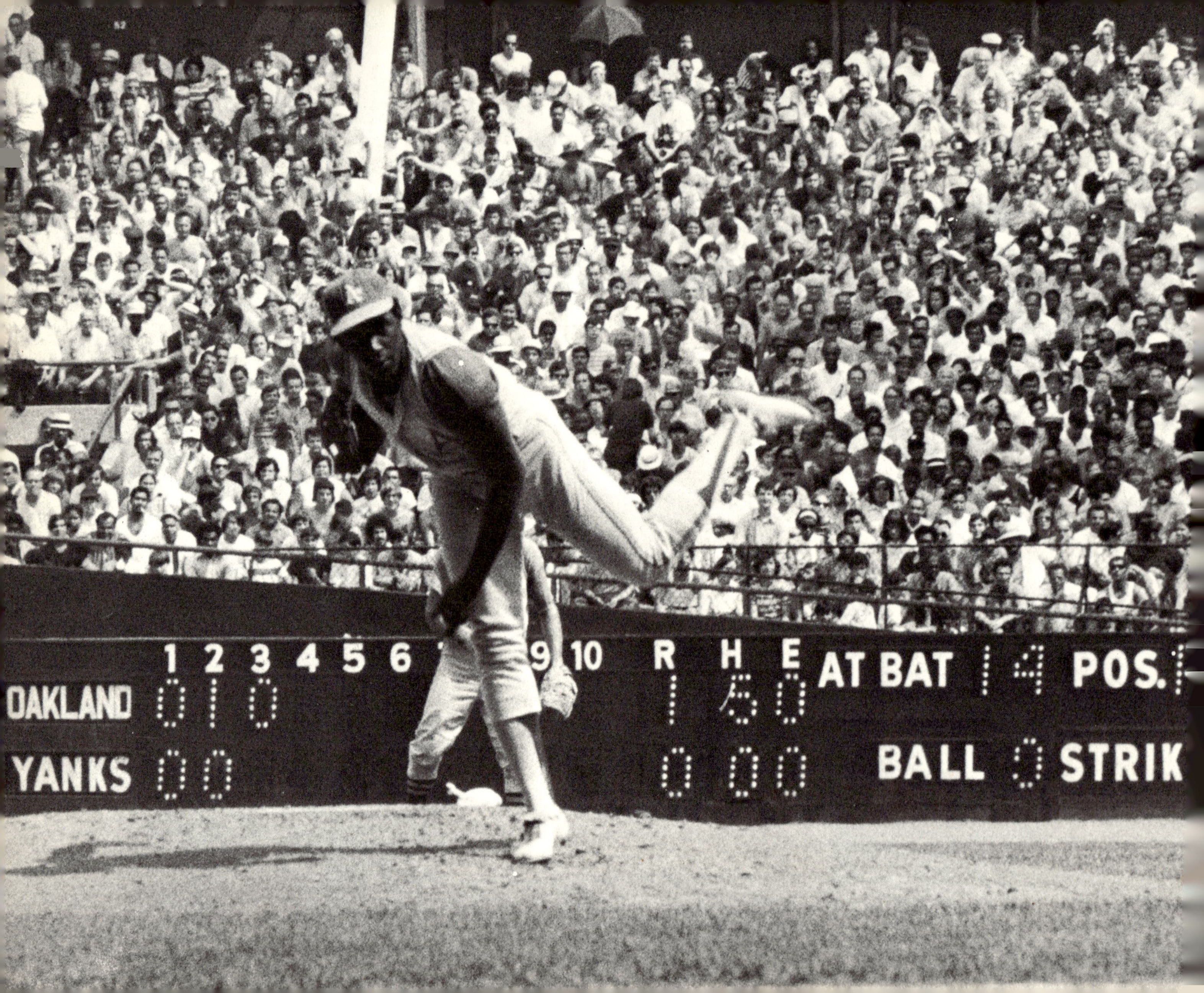
1 2 3 4 5 6
9 10
R H E
AT BAT
POS.
OAKLAND
YANKS
BALL
STRIK

PITCHERS AND PITCHING

George Sullivan

Illustrated with photographs and diagrams

DODD, MEAD & COMPANY
New York

PICTURE CREDITS

Atlanta Braves, 48; F. N. M. Brown, University of Notre Dame, 57; California Angels, 83; Denver Bears, 27; Detroit Tigers, 11; *Harper's Weekly*, 13; Houston Astros, 89; Kansas City Royals, 31 (right); Los Angeles Dodgers, 116; Montreal Expos, 91; National Baseball Library, 107, 109, 110, 112, 114; New York Public Library, 12, 16; Pittsburgh Pirates, 87, 88. All other photographs are by George Sullivan.

FRONTISPIECE: *Baseball's best young pitcher in years — Vida Blue of the Oakland Athletics.*

Copyright © 1972 by George Sullivan
All rights reserved
No part of this book may be reproduced in any form without permission in writing from the publisher
ISBN: 0-396-06473-6
Library of Congress Catalog Card Number: 70-175307
Printed in the United States of America

ACKNOWLEDGMENTS

The author wishes to express his appreciation to many people who assisted him by providing source material and photographs for use in this book. Special thanks are offered the following: Bob Fishel, Vice President, Public Relations, and Clyde Kluttz, Field Director, Player Development, New York Yankees; John Redding, National Baseball Library, National Baseball Hall of Fame; Larry Wigge, *The Sporting News*; Seymour Siwoff, Elias Sports Bureau; Mickey McConnell, Director of Training, Little League Baseball; William J. Guilfoyle, Pittsburgh Pirates; Larry Chaisson, Montreal Expos; Ed Munson, California Angels; Bob Wirz, Kansas City Royals; Hal Middlesworth, Detroit Tigers; Wayne Chandler, Houston Astros; A. E. Patterson, Los Angeles Dodgers; Sy Berger, Sports Director, Topps Chewing Gum, Inc.; Bill Haber; Herb Field, Straight-edge Art Studios; and Conrad Brown.

CONTENTS

"It's 90 Per Cent of the Game"	9	Relief Pitching	71
The Pitcher: A Profile	18	Catchers	77
Up from the Little Leagues	22	The Pitching Coach	83
The Delivery	29	Training and Conditioning	86
The Standard Pitches	36	Pitching Statistics	92
The Specialty Pitches	46	Great Days in Pitching	96
How the Ball Curves	55	The Greatest Pitchers	107
Control	60	All-Time Pitching Records	117
Pitching Strategy	62	Index	121
The Book	66		

Bob Gibson, baseball's standout pitcher of the late 1960's and early 1970's.

"IT'S 90 PER CENT OF THE GAME"

Bob Gibson of the St. Louis Cardinals, baseball's standout pitcher of the late 1960's and early 1970's, played third base in high school, caught, and pitched occasionally. At Creighton University, Gibson played the outfield and pitched. It was there that he decided to concentrate on pitching exclusively.

"I felt I could get to the major leagues fastest as a pitcher," Gibson has said. "Outfielders are a dime a dozen unless you're Willie Mays."

It's true—pitchers *are* special.

If baseball were, like football, thought of in terms of offense and defense, the pitcher would be the offense. He does the attacking. Even the mightiest of of home-run hitters must stand and wait for the pitcher to deliver the ball. He can only react to whatever the pitcher decides to do, a strictly defensive posture.

Some people say that pitching is 75 per cent of baseball. Others claim the figure may be as high as 90 per cent. Look at the game results on any given day. The teams that have the best pitching are the ones that win, almost always. And over the course of a season, the team that has the most effective pitching wins the pennant.

Pitchers are even more of a factor nowadays than they used to be. They are bigger and stronger. They know more about the art and craft of pitching than their predecessors did. They begin younger, at eight or nine in Little Leagues, and by the time they're high school seniors, they may have had as much as ten years of experience. Coaching is better all along the way, especially in the schools.

Being bigger, stronger, and more canny means that everything the pitcher throws is more effective. The fastball is faster. The curve has more zest. Then add the slider, which, to the dismay of batters, continues to increase in popularity, the spitter, which more than a few pitchers throw, the knuckler, screwball, forkball, and all the rest, and you have plenty of reasons for the prevalence of disgruntled .220 hitters.

A strict division of labor is another reason for the pitcher's increased eminence. Today a team's staff consists of four or five starters, a couple of long relief men who are capable of going six or seven innings, and at least two short relievers, rubber-armed throwers who may see action in as many as fifty or sixty games a year. These relief men are experts in their field, not inexperienced youngsters or sore-armed veterans, as used to be the case.

Today's scheduling works in the pitcher's favor. There are more games nowadays (162 of them), at more different times (day, night, and twi-night), in more cities (22 cities as of 1972) than was the case a generation ago. The strain this imposes is felt to a greater degree by the hitters, who play every day. Starting pitchers, of course, rest four days out of every five.

The superiority of the pitchers reached crisis proportions in 1968, a year that has come to be known as "The Year of the Pitcher." Glance at the statistics. The hitters were out to lunch.

Don Drysdale of the Dodgers pitched six shutouts in a row to break a 64-year-old record. During the span he snapped the great Walter Johnson's string of scoreless innings by hurling 58⅔ innings of shutout ball. Denny McLain, then with Detroit, became baseball's first 30-game winner since 1931. Juan Marichal of the San Francisco Giants led the National League with a 26-9 record and 30 complete games. Bob Gibson posted an earned run average of 1.12, establishing a modern record. (A pitcher's earned run average, abbreviated ERA, is often used as a yardstick for measuring his effectiveness. The complete term is "earned run average per nine-inning game," an "earned run" being one for which the pitcher is held responsible. Naturally, the lower one's ERA, the better.)

Only six batsmen reached the .300 mark in 1968, five of them in the National League. Carl Yastrzemski was the lone .300 hitter in the American League, and he finished the season at .301, the lowest figure for a batting champion in history.

Something had to be done. After mulling over a number of different suggestions, baseball officials decided to pare down the size of the strike zone and lower the pitcher's mound. In 1968 the mound was

Juan Marichal of the Giants . . .

fifteen inches high (as measured from the level of the base lines). This may not seem exactly towering, but with Bob Gibson atop it blurring fastballs in, the mound resembled an alpine cliff—at least, batters said it did. Baseball's rulemakers lopped five inches off the mound, and batters began smiling again.

There was nothing unusual about these changes. All of baseball history has been marked by such modifications, as the rulesmakers have sought to maintain the delicate balance between the pitcher and the hitter, the offense and the defense. The intent of the changes was not unusual either, for seldom are rule revisions ever in the pitcher's favor.

How old is the game of baseball itself? The answers vary. Organized baseball claims to be slightly more than a century old, tracing its beginnings to 1869, the year the first team composed entirely of professionals was signed to full-season contracts.

Some people cling to the belief that 1839 should be regarded as the year of baseball's founding. That was the year that Abner Doubleday, later to serve as a Union general in the Civil War, was supposed to have staked out the first baseball diamond on a cow pasture near Cooperstown, New York. Doubleday was regarded as the "inventor" of baseball for

. . . and Denny McLain of the Tigers helped make 1968 "The Year of the Pitcher."

years, and the fact that organized baseball saw fit to establish its Hall of Fame and Museum at Cooperstown and dub the baseball diamond there "Doubleday Field" did much to perpetuate the myth.

"Myth" is the proper word. Research in recent decades has shown that baseball's beginnings are undeniably English. A game in which a ball was pitched and batted, a game with bases and fielders, was played in England during the eighteenth century, and brought by colonists to this country. In some parts of England the game was known as "rounder"; in others it was called "feeder," and in still others the name "base-ball" was used. Evidence of this is *A Little Pretty Pocket-Book,* published in London in 1744. A page in the book said:

BASE-BALL

The ball once struck off,
Away flies the boy
To the next destined post
And then home with joy.

The game as we know it today did not begin to take shape until the 1840's. A group of well-to-do New Yorkers, the Knickerbockers by name, often spent their leisure hours playing a bat and ball game on a diamond-shaped infield with nine-man teams opposing one another. The Knickerbocker who did the most to refine the rules was Alexander Cartwright. A surveyor by profession, Cartwright established foul lines, set the bases ninety feet apart, and, most important, abolished the rule that a batter could be put out by hitting him with the ball as he ran the bases. This change made it possible to introduce a hard ball, and this, in turn, endowed the game with more drama and excitement than it had ever known. "Not until then did baseball go adult— or, if one prefers, did it become a game played by

This verse from A Little Pretty Pocket-Book, published in 1744, is evidence of baseball's English origins.

An early baseball "match" at the Elysian Fields, Hoboken, New Jersey.

grown men as well as boys," says Douglass Wallop in his knowledgeable account of the game, *Baseball, An Informal History.*

Cartwright's rules helped trigger a period of lusty growth for the sport. There were teams composed of barkeepers and firemen, doctors and school teachers, and even clergymen, and they sprang up everywhere. They all had one thing in common; they were all amateur teams.

The era of professionalism is said to have dawned with the Cincinnati Red Stockings of 1869, the game's first pro team. Since they were also the *only* professional team, the Red Stockings' competition consisted of amateur clubs, and they traveled the length and breadth of what was then the United States in quest of opponents. They achieved astounding success. Of the 65 games the Red Stockings played, they won 64, and the only game they didn't win was a tie. Some of their victories were won by incredible margins. They beat the Cincinnati Buckeyes, 103-8. They downed the San Francisco Atlantics, 76-5, the game being mercifully called at the end of five innings.

One reason for the high scores was the rule that restricted the pitcher. Although he was stationed closer to the plate than he is today—45 feet vs. 60½ feet—he was not allowed to swing his arm above hip level in delivering the ball. In other words, he had to pitch underhand. And what was even more prejudicial, he had to put the ball right where the batter wanted it. Henry Chadwick, who wrote extensively about baseball and was an important early influence upon the game, described pitching rules in the 1875 season in a booklet titled, *Dime Baseball Player*. Wrote Chadwick: "The batsman, on taking his position, must call for either a 'high ball,' a 'low ball,' or a 'fair ball' and the umpire shall notify the pitcher to deliver the ball as required. . . . A high ball shall be one sent in above the waist of the batsman but not higher than the shoulders. A low ball shall be one sent in not lower than within one foot of the ground but not higher than the waist. A fair ball shall be one between the range of shoulder high and one foot from the ground. All of the above must be *over the home base.*"

Baseball's first star was a graceful, mustachioed, and bearded gentleman named Harry Wright. Born in England, Wright was a cricket professional with a team that played its games at Elysian Fields at Hoboken, New Jersey, where the Knickerbockers played baseball, and there he learned the game. He became the team captain of the Cincinnati Red Stockings of 1869, played the outfield and also pitched. He was hailed for his braininess or, as one contemporary writer expressed it, "his ability to throw his head up to the plate."

Wright also counseled people of the day who were interested in organizing teams, and many sources call him the "Father of Baseball." (The name has also been applied to Abner Doubleday and Henry Chadwick.) It was as a field leader that Wright received the highest praise. Quiet and patient, he set high standards of conduct for the game. He chided the Philadelphia Athletics, champions in 1871, for displaying their pennant in a saloon. When one of his players struck out or committed an error, Wright's words of reproof usually were, "You need a little ginger." Wright organized the first professional team in Boston, the Red Stockings, and led them to the championship of the National Association from 1872-1875.

Pitchers were humbled in 1881 by a rule that increased the pitching distance to 50 feet. Then the pendulum began to swing the other way for a change. Many of the restrictions that applied to the method of delivering the ball were lifted. Once overhand pitching was permitted, pitchers quickly came to dominate the game.

There was, for instance, Charles (Old Hoss) Radbourn, whose achievements in 1883 make the most gaudy attainments of Bob Gibson seem quite ordinary by comparison. Radbourn, who pitched for Providence in the National League (which had been founded in 1876), won 44 and lost 28 that year. He was warming up. The next season he posted a 60-12 record, including 11 shutouts. His earned run average was 0.99.

That year, 1884, the first World Series, pitting

FIG. 8. STRAIGHT DELIVERY.

Grasp the ball securely between the first and second fingers with the thumb on the opposite side, the other fingers being closed in the palm of the hand. Deliver the ball to the batsman with all possible speed, either by a straight throw from the shoulder or by an underhand throw at a level with the waist. In this, as well as all other deliveries of the ball, the pitcher should exert himself to retain absolute command of the ball if possible.

FIG. 9 OUT-CURVE.

Secure the ball in the hand by pressing it firmly between the first two fingers and the thumb, with the third and little fingers closed in the palm of the hand. In delivering the ball to the batsman throw the arm forward midway between the shoulder and waist, and at the moment of releasing the ball, turn or twist the hand quickly to the left.

Henry Chadwick gave this instructional advice to pitchers in his book, *The Art of Pitching*, published in 1885.

Providence against the old New York Metropolitans of the American Association, was played, and Radbourn was the star. It was contested on a three-games-out-of-five basis, but five games weren't necessary. Old Hoss, pitching on successive days, won all three.

Radbourn was no isolated case. Jim Galvin won 46 games for Buffalo of the National League in

These are the Boston Red Stockings of 1874. Captain Harry Wright is seated, center. His brother George, the team's shortstop and perhaps the best fielder of the day, is seated in front of Harry and to his right. A. G. Spalding, the Boston pitcher, stands behind Harry and to his left. A control and change-of-pace pitcher, Spalding won 221 games in a five-year period beginning in 1872.

1883, and he also played the outfield that year. Timothy (Smiling Tim) Keefe won 42 games for the National League's New York Giants in 1886, and two years later, on his way to a 35-20 record, won 19 in a row.

The batter's eminence was restored in 1893 when the pitching slab was moved back to its present distance—60½ feet. "The object of the change," said an early guide book, "was to increase the batting, handicap the pitcher, and add to the interest of the sport."

The new rule was immediately effective. Twelve men had hit .300 or better in 1892; 60 did in 1893. Said the guide book: "In many notable instances pitchers were driven out of the business, or their effectiveness was so weakened as to make them of little or no worth to their respective clubs."

Little by little, pitchers grew accustomed to the new distance, and by the early 1900's low-scoring games were once again as common as complaints about training camp food. In 1905 Elmer Flick won the American League batting title with a .306 average, and J. Franklin (Home-Run) Baker was able to earn a reputation as a slugger and a niche in the Hall of Fame by winning the home-run championship in four consecutive years with a *total* of 39.

Another reason that pitchers of this period were clearly superior to batters was because the rules did nothing to prevent them from tampering with the cover of the ball. They could spit on it if they wanted to. They could scuff it up with emery cloth, nick it with a knife, or unravel a stitch or two with a razor blade. It wasn't until 1920 that the ball was made sacred; pitchers were then prevented from doing anything to doctor it or dampen it.

The year before, 1919, a chunky young star named Babe Ruth, who played for the Boston Red Sox, broke the all-time home-run record by hitting 29. The next year he was traded to the Yankees and hit 54. It was not the change of scenery that boosted Ruth's total. It was the ball. It had been made much more livelier. The game would never be the same.

Modern baseball dates from this time. The souped-up ball forced infielders to field the ball differently. They had to glove it quickly and cleanly and be set to throw as soon as it was secure in their grasp. Hitters no longer wanted just singles. The home run, or at least the extra base hit, became the aim of every man who stepped to the plate. That was fine with the owners. Home runs were what brought people to the ball parks.

Pitchers adjusted, too. The delivery became simpler. Before the days of the lively ball, the pitcher's windup and delivery had been terribly intricate, sometimes more perplexing to the batter than the pitch that evolved from it. But the friskier ball came back so hard and so fast that the pitcher had to abandon his involved windup in favor of one that would allow him to end up with both feet solidly planted, ready to field the cannon's shot. New pitches were introduced. The prominence of the slider can be traced to this period.

The task of fooling the batter is not easy, and the men who make the rules often seem intent on making it more and more difficult. They have made the ball bouncier. They have made the pitcher throw it farther and farther. In recent years, they have cut the size of his target area and shaved down the mound from which he works.

Yet somehow the pitcher has always managed to adjust to the discriminatory treatment. He has always overcome.

THE PITCHER: A PROFILE

WANTED—YOUNG MAN WITH A TALENT FOR DELIVERING A BASEBALL TO A BATTER. WORK EVERY FIFTH DAY FROM APRIL TO OCTOBER. FIRST CLASS TRAVEL AND LIVING ACCOMMODATIONS. ALL EXPENSES PAID. MINIMUM SALARY, $12,500, BONUS ARRANGEMENTS. LIBERAL PENSION PLAN. INQUIRE AT YOUR LOCAL MAJOR LEAGUE CLUB.

No wonder so many thousands of young men want to be major league pitchers. The pay is admirable. The work is "play" and, when you think about it, it isn't *that* difficult. Essentially, it involves the skill of being able to deliver a 5.2-ounce baseball within a 17-inch-wide strike zone from a distance of 60½ feet, and do it with accuracy 110 to 115 times in a game once or twice a week. Children of nine or ten can do it.

Yet of the thousands upon thousands of young men who call themselves pitchers, only a handful achieve any degree of eminence. Each major league team carries nine or ten, which means there is a total of less than 250.

What special qualities do these men have?

Good size is one. Virtually all major league pitchers are 6-foot-1 to 6-foot-3 in height, and several scale 6-foot-6. The average weight is 200 pounds plus.

Their method of delivering the ball varies. Some come straight overhand with it. Others sidearm; still others employ a three-quarter overhand style.

Some pitchers rely on the fastball. They have a good curve and good control, but they are exceptionally fast, so they use their speed to overpower hitters.

Then there are "stuff" pitchers. They feature an array of breaking pitches thrown at different speeds. They are also noted for good control. Many of them have a specialty pitch, a knuckle ball, a forkball, or even a spitball, which they use as their money pitch.

Finally, there are pitchers whose forte is strategy. Like the stuff pitchers, they have a variety of breaking pitches and control the ball well, but their principal weapon is their craftiness.

What makes the major league pitcher special is something more than his skill in delivering the ball and the ability he has to control it, to put it exactly where he wants. It's something inside the man.

The best pitchers are rugged competitors. They work hard, and not just when they happen to be pitching. To keep in condition, they do plenty of running between starts. They are constantly counseling with their coaches and teammates to improve their knowledge of the batters they must face. They throw a great deal, in a continual effort to better the quality of their pitches and their control or in an effort to add to their repertoire.

Confidence is another hallmark of the topflight

Bob Gibson has won a prominent place in baseball's record book.

pitcher. He never hesitates to challenge a hitter, even the best. In a critical situation he will throw his best pitch, and he will keep throwing it even if in the back of his mind he knows the hitter will tee off on it if it's not thrown exactly right.

In recent years, Bob Gibson of the St. Louis Cardinals has served as the standard against which other pitchers are measured. A fierce competitor, indeed, a man with a deep hatred of losing, Gibson's records and achievements are so numerous they require an entire page in the *Baseball Register*, the sport's official record manual.

Gibson's blazing fastball and hard slider have earned him the National League's Cy Young Memorial Award twice. In 1968, a year he was named the league's Most Valuable Player, Gibson turned in a record-setting 1.12 earned run average. In 1970 he became the first pitcher in major league history to attain a total of 200 or more strikeouts for eight seasons.

He has been brilliant in World Series play. He pitched nine games in three series and completed every game. He won seven consecutive games—a record—and also set three strike-out marks: 17 strikeouts in one game, 35 in a series, and 92 in 81 innings.

Gibson doesn't excel simply as a thrower. He is probably the best all-around performer of recent times. He is a fine hitter, and during one season he drove in 20 runs—more than any other pitcher, yes, but also more than any pitching *staff*. Gibson has also achieved considerable eminence as a fielder. In four consecutive years, beginning in 1965, he won the Golden Glove Award as the best fielding pitcher in the National League. *Sport* Magazine once called him, "An extra shortstop in the field, cat-quick, sure-handed . . ."

Gibson's skills are matched by his tenacity and "true grit." In 1967 a line drive off the bat of Roberto Clemente fractured the fibula, the shin bone, of Bob's right leg. But before Gibson came out of the game, he pitched to three more batters, an incredible display of courage. "I've never come out of a game on my own," he once said. *"Never."*

Tom Seaver, who won 25 games in 1969 in leading the New York Mets to their first pennant, is another of today's pitchers with an enormous will to win. Seaver has a sizzling fastball, an array of curves, and a fine slider. He is a determined hitter, an alert fielder, and a heady baserunner. That's not all. "He's the leader of the team," says Met shortstop Bud Harrelson. "He knows when to pop off. He knows when to needle a guy. He's the one who keeps us on our toes."

Early in his career, Seaver pitched against the Phillies, a game watched by Robin Roberts, one of Philadelphia's all-time pitching greats. In the seventh

Tom Seaver's will to win has paid dividends. Here he receives his championship ring from commissioner Bowie Kuhn.

inning, Seaver drew a base on balls, stole second, went to third on a wild pitch, and scampered home on an infield out. The run he scored was the Mets' margin of victory. After the game, a reporter asked Roberts his opinion of Seaver's performance.

Roberts smiled. "Look at the scoreboard," he said. "There's your answer. He wins. He'll do anything to beat you."

Competitiveness—that's what separates the best pitchers from the rest. They hate to give up a hit, even if they are six runs behind. Losing kills them.

Pittsburgh fastballer Dock Ellis has proven a rugged competitor.

UP FROM THE LITTLE LEAGUES

If a rookie loses his first start as a major league pitcher, newspaper accounts of the game are likely to cite the young man's nervousness and lack of experience. Nervousness may be one reason for the loss, but lack of experience usually isn't. By the time a pitcher reaches the big leagues, he's likely to have pretty well mastered his art. Although he may be only twenty or twenty-one years old, he has well over a decade of experience behind him.

With most players, it all begins with the Little Leagues. Founded in Williamsport, Pennsylvania, in 1939, Little League baseball originally involved only youngsters eight to twelve years old, but it now includes teams in age groups up to eighteen. After World War II, Little Leagues spread throughout the United States and were introduced in foreign countries. In 1971, 8,593 Little Leagues were in operation in thirty-one different countries, with more than one million youngsters taking part in the competition.

After Little League competition, tens of thousands of youngsters go on to Babe Ruth baseball. In 1971 there were almost 250,000 teen-agers participating in this two-division program. The greatest number were members of the thirteen to fifteen age group, while the remainder were active in the sixteen to eighteen division.

Babe Ruth baseball was founded in 1951 in Ham-

Little League play has been the starting point for countless major league pitchers.

ilton Township, a suburb of Trenton, New Jersey, and spread quickly throughout the United States. Today, Babe Ruth Leagues are flourishing in all fifty states, Canada, Puerto Rico, Mexico, and parts of Europe and Asia.

More than one hundred major league players are graduates of Babe Ruth baseball, including some of the game's most notable pitchers. Tom Seaver and Jim Palmer, starting pitchers for their respective leagues in the 1970 All Star game, Dave McNally, Mickey Lolich, Mel Stottlemyre, Fritz Peterson, and Denny McLain are among the front-line pitchers who list Babe Ruth baseball as part of their experience.

The experience and training that youngsters receive as teenagers is probably more important than any other. As Little League players, they are usually not mature enough either physically or emotionally to learn a great deal. About all you can teach a boy of nine or ten is how to stand on the mound and how to deliver the ball, say coaches.

It is when he reaches high school that the significant instruction begins. "This is the important age," says Clyde Kluttz, Field Director, Player Development, of the New York Yankees. "This is where the boy begins to get the muscles he should develop properly, the long, loose, supple muscles that are so important. A high school pitcher can actually develop his fastball and begin developing his curve."

College baseball is of only limited value as far as the young pitcher is concerned. The season is short, since it is restricted to the spring months, and the boy may receive only seven or eight pitching opportunities.

Any high school pitcher of more than average skill is sure to attract the attention of the major league talent scouts. Pitchers are the easiest players to scout. The first thing the scout looks for is a strong arm, the ability to throw hard. This skill can't be taught. "If a fellow sixteen to eighteen can't throw the ball hard, he won't be able to develop a fastball that will win for him in the majors" says a former scout for the Los Angeles Dodgers. "Fingering and changing his style can be worked on by your coaches, but you can't take a 'softballer,' as I used to call them, and by coaching make him a fastball pitcher."

The scout also determines whether the young prospect has a curveball and change-up, and assesses his ability to control the ball. He also appraises the young man's character and temperament. Is he confident? Is he determined? Does he have the willingness to learn and the intelligence to learn quickly? Does he have the capacity to bounce back after a defeat?

Many high school graduates become caught up

The shortness of the season limits the value of college baseball.

MINNESOTA TWINS BASEBALL CLUB

PLAYER INFORMATION CARD

NAME _____ (Last) _____ (First) _____ (Middle)
POSITION _____
BATS _____ HGT. _____
THROWS _____ WGT. _____

ADDRESS _____ (Number) _____ (Street) _____ (City) _____ (P.O. Zone) _____ (State)
DATE OF BIRTH _____ (Month) _____ (Day) _____ (Year)
TELEPHONE _____
PARENT'S NAME _____
NAME AND ADDRESS OF HIGH SCHOOL OR COLLEGE _____
DATE OF YOUR GRADUATION FROM HIGH SCHOOL OR COLLEGE _____ (Month) _____ (Day) _____ (Year)
ARE YOU A MEMBER OF AN AMERICAN LEGION JUNIOR TEAM? _____
HAVE YOU EVER SIGNED A PROFESSIONAL BASEBALL CONTRACT? _____ (When) _____ (What Club)
ARE YOU NOW A FREE AGENT? _____ MILITARY STATUS _____

PHYSICAL DESCRIPTION (BUILD, SIZE, AGILITY, ETC.) _____
HABITS _____
CLASSIFICATION IN WHICH SHOULD PLAY NEXT YEAR: _____
PLAYER RECOMMENDED BY: _____ REPORT BY: _____ DATE _____

SCOUT REPORT SECTION

CLUB & LEAGUE _____
LENGTH OF OBSERVATION _____
ARM _____ ACCURACY _____
FIELDING _____
HITTING _____ POWER _____
RUNNING SPEED _____ BASE RUNNING _____
PITCHER { SPEED _____
CURVE _____
CHANGE _____
CONTROL _____ }
APTITUDE _____ REACTIONS _____
AGGRESSIVENESS _____
DEFINITE PROSPECT? _____
HAS CHANCE? _____
OTHER REMARKS: _____

Scouts for the Minnesota Twins use this form in appraising prospects.

in the free-agent draft, which baseball initiated in 1965. Teams draft the "rights" to negotiate with players they have scouted. There are two drafts each year, one in June, the other in January. If a young man does not sign with the club that has drafted him, his name goes back into the pool for the next draft. The process keeps repeating itself until one of three alternatives is reached: (1) he signs with the club which has drafted him; (2) he enrolls in a four-year college (in which case he cannot be drafted until he graduates); or (3) he passes his twenty-first birthday.

Before the days of the free-agent draft, teams bid in unrestrained fashion for playing talent. Bonus payments sometimes reached the stratosphere. The classic example is Rick Reichardt who signed with

PITCHERS	THR	AGE	HGT.	WGT.	FB/M	CRV	CON	XP/?	FIELD	EXP	PROS	DRAFT
MORRELL, BILL	L	21	6'1"	180	G/-	G	-			1	NO	
KRAWIECKI, JOHN	R	22	6'2"	185	G/-	-	-	sldr/-		2	NO	
GARCIA, RALPH	R	22	6'1"	185	G/-	∤	-			1	NO	
BIELSKI, DAN	R	22	6'1"	190	-/-	-	-	chg/-		2	NO	
ALBURY, VIC	L	23	6'	180	-/G	G	-	chg/G		2	NO	
KATAWCZIK, FRED	L	23	6'4"	200	-/-	-	-			4	NO	
HARDY, LARRY	R	22	5'10"	180	G/G	-	G	sldr/G		1	NO	
PRESTON, JOHN	R	19	6'3"	170	∤/G		P			1	NO	
GREEN, JOHN	R	24	6'3"	205	∤/G	-	-	sldr/G		4	chance	NO

A scout for the St. Louis Cardinals made this evaluation of nine young pitchers; one was given a "chance."

the California Angels in 1964 for a bonus of $175,000. The free-agent draft, by putting an end to competitive bidding for playing talent, put a lid on bonus payments. Before the draft was instituted, the No. 1 selection could expect a bonus of upwards of $150,000. Afterward, he had to be content with less than half that amount.

The free-agent draft also diminished the importance of baseball's scouts. Before the draft, teams employed scouts to ferret out and evaluate baseball talent. In addition, each scout was expected to convince a young prospect that he should sign with the team that the scout represented.

With the free-agent draft in effect, this last-named responsibility was eliminated. A boy became important only to the team that drafted him. Nowadays the role of the scout is limited to watching a prospect a few times, assessing his talents, and then filing a report to the club. Then it is up to the front office to decide whether or not to draft the young man. Before the draft, some clubs had as many as thirty or forty scouts. Now they have less than half that number.

Some young men prefer to wait until they have graduated from college before embarking on a major league career. But no matter what route a prospect chooses, virtually no one goes directly from amateur competition into the major leagues. There is always a stopover in the minor leagues.

Approximately 3,500 to 4,000 players participate in minor league baseball, or, to use the official name, The National Association of Professional Baseball Leagues. Ninety-nine per cent of all major leaguers active today have had minor league experience.

A pitcher learns how to think in the minor leagues. He learns how to become a winning pitcher. He learns control.

"Many young pitchers come out of high school and go into professional ball, and some of them can really pitch," says Mickey Lolich of the Detroit Tigers. "They can throw the ball right through a brick wall—but the problem is they can't hit the brick wall. The minor leagues are where a pitcher learns how to pitch, how to throw over the plate,

Hometown fans watch the Denver Bears. Ninety-nine per cent of major league players have had minor league experience.

how to change speeds. He learns everything there about getting the hitter out.

"A lot of kids have never had to taste defeat in their lives. But in the minor leagues, if you're a pitcher, you're going to start to lose ball games. You're not as good as you thought you were, and the guys you're playing against are giving you better competition. You've got to learn to lose as well as how to win. It makes a man out of you."

The parent club watches its minor league players carefully. Every strike a pitcher throws, every ball, every winning game and every loss is noted in the player's record. If a boy impresses the management he is moved up to a league where the competition is stronger. Usually several years of minor league seasoning are necessary. Then one winter day the boy receives a letter telling him to report to the major league training camp the next spring. The great adventure is about to begin. Combining both his amateur and professional experience, it has taken about ten years to reach the starting point.

The Pirates' Dave Giusti comes through straight overhand.

THE DELIVERY

Every pitcher winds up and delivers the ball in a manner that best suits his physical make-up. A stocky pitcher like Andy Messersmith can't kick his leg high in the air like tall, slim Lindy McDaniel or the lithe Juan Marichal.

While there is no standard way of delivering the ball, methods of delivery are classified as being either overhand, sidearm, or in-between, a delivery that's three-quarters overhand. There is also the underhand or "submarine" method, but this is seldom seen.

Coaches and managers prefer to see a young pitcher use the overhand delivery because it puts less strain on the arm than any of the others. It is usually used by pitchers who throw the fastest. It is the type of delivery that makes for a fastball that rises, that "rides" or "tails-up."

Three-quarter and sidearm deliveries give the right-handed pitcher an advantage over the right-handed batter because he gets only a quick look at the pitcher's arm motion and release. The left-handed batter gets a longer look, which is one reason lefties do better against right-handed pitchers. A pitch thrown by a sidearm hurler does not rise; it breaks down.

Ted Abernathy of the Kansas City Royals was one of the few pitchers in recent years who was successful with the underhand style. He threw a sinking fastball and rising curve. For a change-up, he relied on a knuckle ball.

The pitcher's strength and preliminary windup have little or no effect on the pitch itself. These initial movements may serve to relax him, to loosen his uniform, or to confuse the batter, but they don't serve to make the pitch travel any faster.

In his windup and delivery of the ball, the pitcher must obey basic scientific principles in order to get the ball moving at maximum speed. About three hundred years ago, Sir Isaac Newton, the great English physicist, mathematician, and philosopher, formulated a "law" about motion that said: "An object in motion tends to continue in motion at the same speed and in the same direction, unless some force causes a change." In accord with Newton's law, the faster a pitcher can get the ball moving as he winds up, the faster it will travel to the plate.

He must bring the ball forward in as wide an arc as possible. To achieve this wide arc, he holds the ball back as far as he can at the start of his windup. He gets it back even farther by lifting one leg from the ground, bending the knee of the other leg, and tilting his entire body back.

When he brings the ball forward, his feet act as the center of a large circle, with his legs, trunk, and arm together serving as the circle's radius. He builds arm speed gradually as he brings the ball forward. His delivery has to be smooth and rhythmic from start to finish; he cannot rush.

Ray Sadecki of the Mets whips the ball to the plate in sidearm fashion.

San Diego's Dan Coombs delivers with a three-quarters overhand style.

Ted Abernathy of the Kansas City Royals was successful with a "submarine" method of delivery.

By studying motion pictures, scientists have found that for maximum velocity the ball should leave the pitcher's hand just after the upper arm passes the line of the shoulders. The forearm should be passing just beyond the vertical. When coaches say that the ball should leave the hand "at a point that's level with the peak of the cap," it's the same thing.

The point of release affects not only the speed but accuracy also. If the pitcher releases too early, the pitch will be high. A late release causes the ball to go low.

Another of Newton's laws states: "For every action there is always an equal or contrary reaction." This can be applied to the push-off the pitcher gets from the pitching rubber. The "reaction" from the rubber gives his body extra propulsion which he transmits to his arm and, thus, to the ball.

As a general rule, the taller the pitcher, the greater his capability to throw fast. It's because his extra height and arm length enable him to form a wider arc as he brings the ball forward.

The follow-through, while important, adds nothing to the speed of the pitch. Once the ball leaves the pitcher's hand, only air resistance and gravity's force (and the hitter's bat) affect its flight. The follow-through has the value of putting the pitcher in a position to field a struck ball should it be batted toward him.

One other aspect of the delivery is important—the wrist snap. The pitcher's wrist is bent back as his arm swings through. At the last possible moment he snaps the wrist forward and this further increases the ball's velocity.

Sometimes a pitcher throws with perfection for several innings, and then allows a base hit or perhaps he issues a walk. Suddenly the roof collapses. Singles and doubles, and perhaps worse, are sprayed to every corner of the ball park.

What has happened? What has gone wrong?

With some pitchers the trouble stems from the different motion they must use with a man on base. The rules say that the pitcher cannot take his full windup with a runner on, but must pitch from what the rulebook calls a "set" position. He has to face the batter, his pivot foot in contact with the rubber, holding the ball in both hands in front of his body, and then deliver the ball from this position.

The quick switch from one method of delivery to the other is sometimes upsetting to the pitcher. Besides, the pressure of the baserunner works to annoy him.

A pitcher's delivery is also important to his efficiency as a fielder. If he is winding up and following through correctly, he'll be in a perfect position to field the ball at the end of his delivery.

Fielding bunts is a special art, often closely re-

The different motion a pitcher is required to take with a man on base sometimes causes difficulty. This is Gary Peters of the Red Sox.

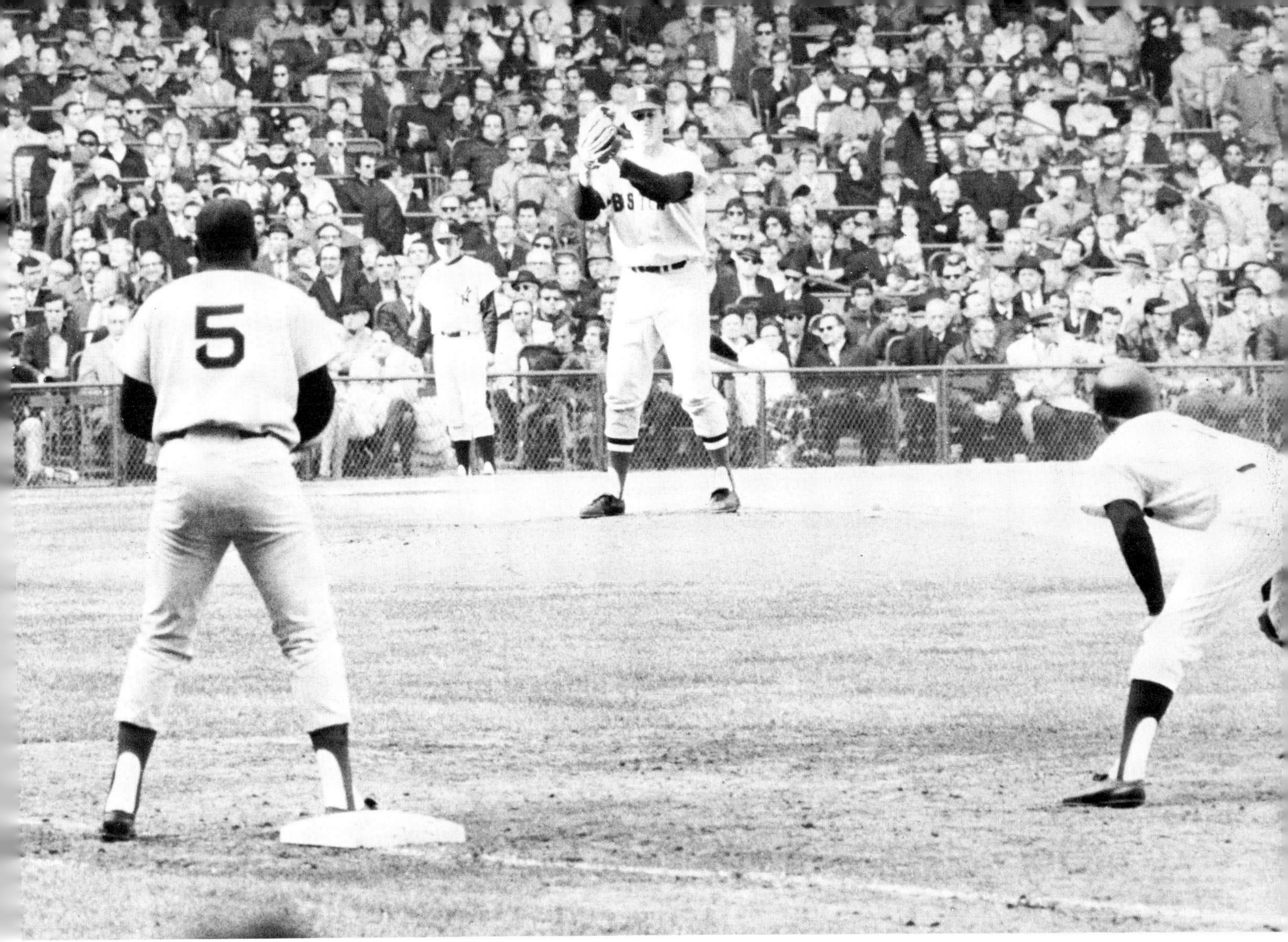

Good fielding is important to winning. Here Ken Tatum breaks left in an effort to grab a drive from the bat of Horace Clarke.

lated to the pitch thrown. In an "automatic" bunting situation—men on first and second—the pitcher knows the batter is going to be trying to bunt toward third base. He may throw a relatively slow pitch that enables the batter to do just this, but the pitcher breaks for the third-base foul line with the release of the ball. He's thus in a good position to make a play at third.

Pitchers have to learn to back up plays, too. On a passed ball or wild pitch, with runners on second or third, the pitcher must cover the plate while the catcher retrieves the ball. When a runner is on second and the batter singles, the pitcher is supposed to back up the catcher. When there is a runner on first and second and the batter singles, the pitcher is supposed to back up the third baseman. Some pitchers are more alert to these responsibilities than others.

A pitcher also has to learn to help himself with the bat. Unfortunately, only a minority do. One reason is that pitchers get to take batting practice only on the day they are going to pitch. Also, every pitcher bears down harder on his opposite number.

It is a matter of fact that the pitcher who can field well and who can hit, as well as deliver the ball effectively, will win an extra game or two over a season. Warren Spahn, who, in his twenty-year major league career, won 363 games—the most ever for a left-hander—was one of the most accomplished all-around performers in baseball history.

Once a teammate of Spahn was asked to explain his success. "He can field his position," the man said. "He can bunt well to either side of the infield. He can hit behind the runner. He can do all these things to beat you—and I haven't even talked about his pitching skills yet."

THE STANDARD PITCHES

To foil batters, most pitchers rely on fastballs and curves thrown at varying speeds. There is a great deal more to pitching strategy than this implies, but fastballs and curves are the core of that strategy.

THE FASTBALL

The fastball is just that, a ball that is delivered with all the velocity a pitcher can muster. The fastball does not, as many people believe, travel a perfectly straight line. It may veer up or down or to the right or left. Batters describe this characteristic by saying that a pitcher's ball has a hop on it or is "moving."

Bob Feller, a former Cleveland pitching great, in 1947 threw a baseball across the plate at 98.6 miles per hour, as measured with electronic instruments. J. G. Taylor Spink, editor of *The Sporting News*, stated that this was the accepted world record for the fastball pitch.

It is not difficult to understand why such a pitch is hard to hit. A ball that shoots to the plate at ninety miles an hour is in the air less than half a second—45/100 of a second to be exact. Only the most gifted batters can react successfully to a pitch traveling at that speed.

Sandy Koufax's speed was often said to be equal to that of Feller's. Among today's pitchers, Bob Gibson is considered to be among the fastest. Baseball men say *the* fastest is Nolan Ryan, a tall, loose-limbed right-hander, signed by the New York Mets in 1965.

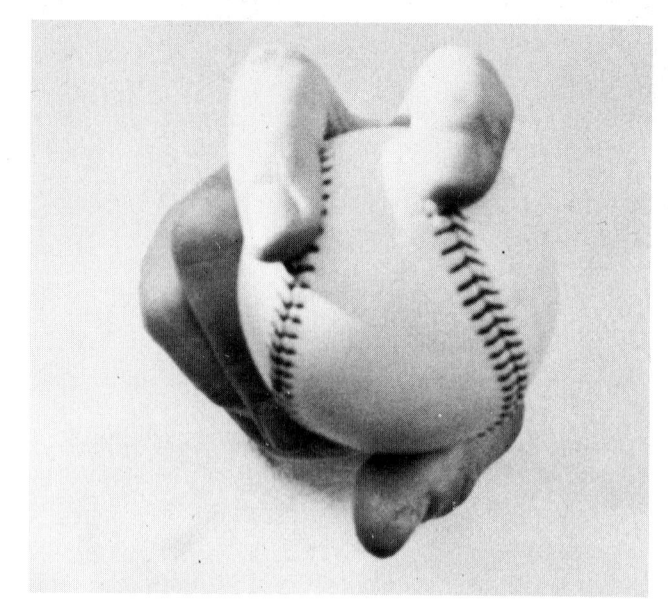

Speed is only part of the difficulty as far as the hitter is concerned. The fact that the ball "moves" complicates things. Just how it moves depends on how the ball is delivered and how it is gripped.

Take the matter of delivery. A pitcher who fires a fastball with an overhand style will throw a ball that

The fastball

Nolan Ryan was said to have baseball's fastest fastball.

has a tendency to rise. A fastball thrown by a right-handed sidearmer veers to the right. And in the case of a right-hander who employs a three-quarter overhand style, the ball both rises and breaks to the right.

The accepted method of gripping a fastball is along the seams at their narrowest point, but this varies from pitcher to pitcher. Most pitchers have a number of ways of gripping. For example, when Bob Gibson wants to throw a fastball that will veer away from a right-handed hitter, he holds the ball across the seams. But when he wants the ball to veer toward a right-hander, he grips it so that the fingers run along the seams.

Some pitchers are said to throw sinking fastballs. This results from another variation in the delivery. To throw a sinker, a right-hander follows through with a downward motion, and rotates his wrist to the left as he releases. Mel Stottlemyre of the New York Yankees is well known for his sinking fastball.

THE CURVE

The second essential pitch is the curve. When thrown overhand by a right-handed pitcher to a right-handed batter, the curve breaks down and away from the man at the plate, with the downwardness of the break its most dominant characteristic. A sidearm right-hander gets only lateral break. By varying the speed of the pitch and the amount of

Mel Stottlemyre throws a sinking fastball.

break, pitchers develop several different curveballs.

Spin is what makes the curveball curve. Most pitchers grip the ball across the seams at the narrowest point. But the grip isn't as critical as the method of release. The pitcher must jerk his hand down in front of his body as he fires, a motion that is often compared to pulling down a window shade. This is what makes the ball spin. Curveball specialist Warren Spahn once said that the ball should roll out of the pitcher's fingers in much the same manner that a boy flips a yo-yo.

A few pitchers throw a knuckle curve. This is a pitch that is spun off the first knuckle of the index finger.

Many people believe that the greater a curveball's break, the more effective it is. Not at all. It's where and when the pitch is thrown that counts. It must be kept low and on the corners. It must be used only when the batter is least expecting it. Coaches agree that more mistakes are made with curves than with any other pitch.

The curve

The knuckle curve

Sometimes a curveball fails to break; it "hangs." It may be that the pitcher failed to jerk his arm down hard enough. Or it might be the opposite, bringing his hand down too hard. The first causes the ball to break too soon, the other too late. Either way it's trouble for the pitcher.

Pitchers have been curving the ball for over a hundred years. William Arthur (Candy) Cummings, who was born in Ware, Massachusetts, in 1848, is

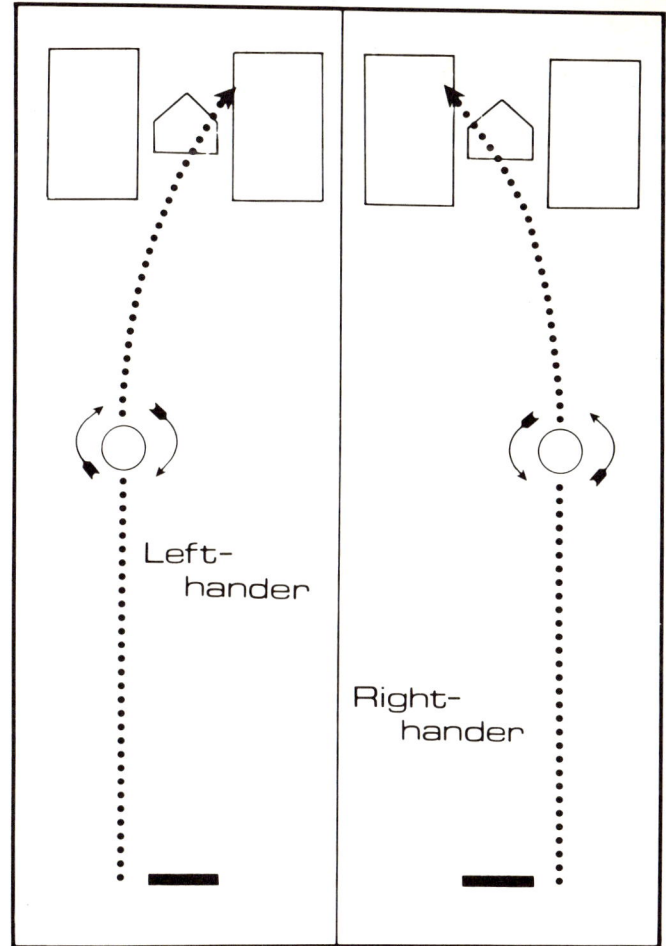

With a left-hander, the curveball spins right and breaks right. With a right-hander, it's just the opposite.

Jerry Koosman of the Mets shows his curveball style.

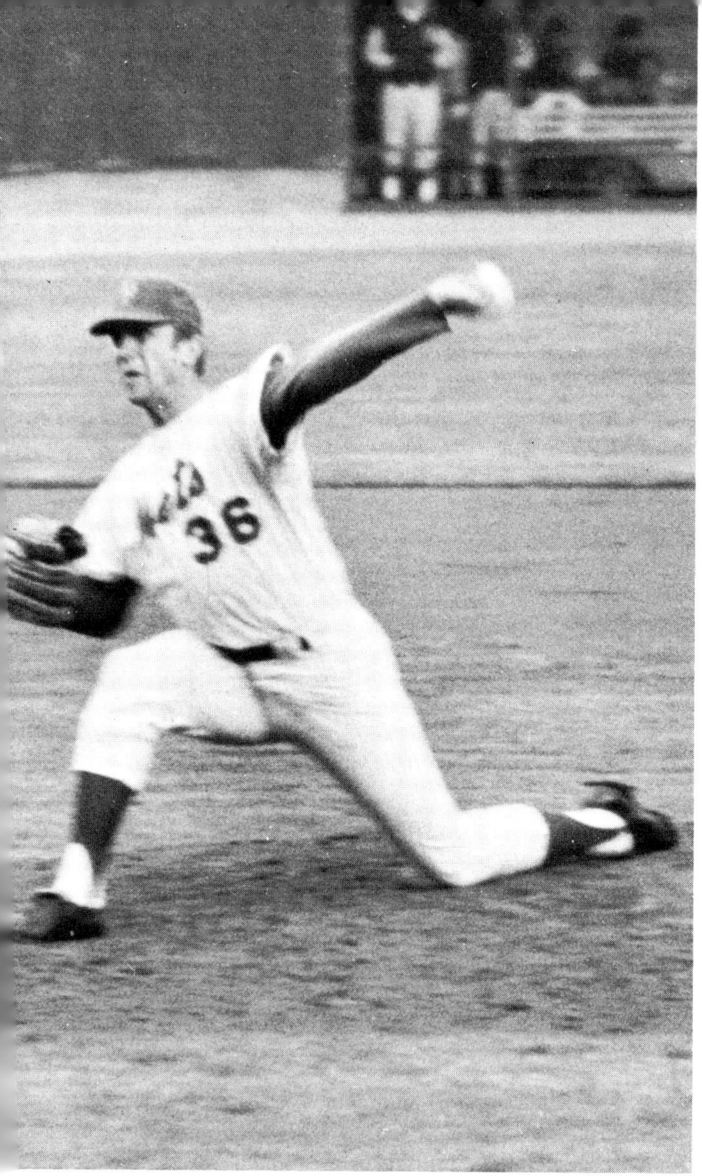
36

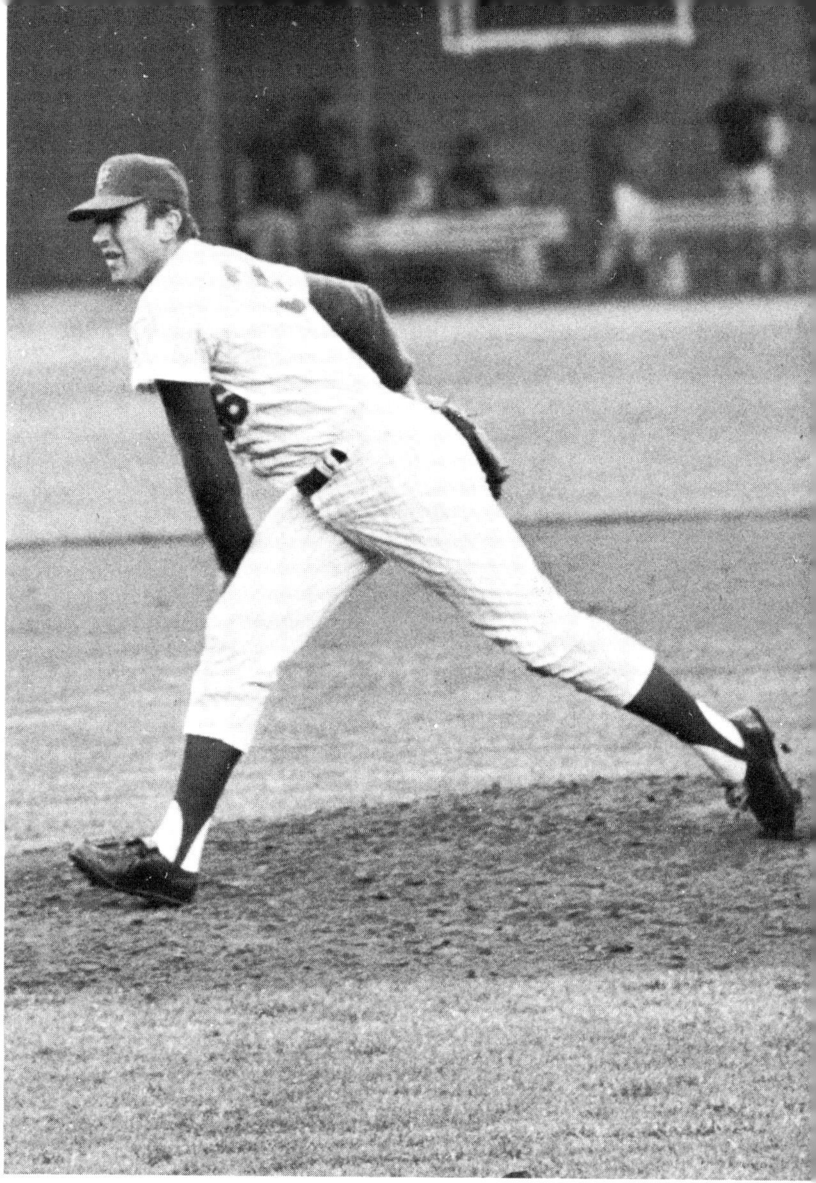

often called the discoverer of the curveball. However, many sources say that pitchers were using it before his time. What Cummings did do was find out what made the ball bend and dip, and then he successfully applied what he learned to his own delivery.

Varying the Speed

Besides being able to throw the ball fast and make it break, a pitcher must also be able to slow down his pitches, to throw a change of pace, sometimes called a "change-up" or simply a "change." The motion used in delivering a change of pace must be exactly the same as the pitcher uses for his fastball or curve. If the batter knows the change-up is coming, it's not going to be effective.

To throw a change-of-pace pitch, the pitcher grips the ball loosely. When he releases, there's no wrist snap. Pitchers develop several shades of slowness for each pitch, varying from half-speed or even slower to three-quarter speed pitches.

Sparky Anderson, manager of the Reds, says that Gary Nolan, one of Cincinnati's starters, throws the best change-up in the league. "I throw it three different ways," Nolan says. "But how I throw it is a secret."

The change-up

The Slider

The slider, a sort of cross between the fastball and curve, has achieved immense popularity in the last ten years or so. The slider looks like a fastball as it approaches the batter, but at the last second it seems to veer—"slide"—a few inches to the left or right with a downward slant. Although the break is slight, it's enough to take the ball out of the bat's range.

The grip for the slider is along one seam. The pitch is thrown with a firm wrist and a "turn of the screw" rotation. It's not like the curveball release, which requires a sharp wrist snap and a flip of the

The Reds' Gary Nolan (right), pictured here with teammate Jim Merritt, is a change-of-pace artist.

first two fingers.

The slider has to be thrown hard. It *must* slide. If it doesn't, it's no more than a fastball that is not traveling very fast, and this has to be disastrous for the pitcher. It is generally agreed that more home runs are hit off the slider than any other pitch—evidence that pitchers often let up on the pitch.

The slider has zoomed in popularity for two reasons: it's easy for a pitcher to throw—Whitey Ford of the Yankees is said to have learned to throw it in just one day—yet the batter has real difficulty trying to determine what it is. He's never quite sure it's not a fastball.

Ted Williams, the great Red Sox slugger and, later, manager of the Washington Senators, once recalled that in his early years in the major league he had only two pitches to worry about—the fastball and the curveball. Since Williams had the reputation of being a good fastball hitter, the curve was virtually the only pitch he had to outguess. But later

The slider

Andy Messersmith has a curve and slider that are about the best in baseball.

in his career, pitchers began throwing him sliders and it made his guesswork much more complicated. Says Williams, who hit .406 in 1941, "The slider has got to be one of the reasons for lower batting averages these days."

Left-hander Dave McNally had an exasperating experience with his slider. When McNally pitched for Elmira in the Eastern League in 1962, his slider was a thing of beauty. The next year McNally joined the Baltimore Orioles, and the pitch deserted him. Whenever he tried it, the ball's break was feeble. He had to discard the pitch.

One day in spring training in 1968, when McNally was throwing to catcher Andy Etchebarren, McNally signalled a short curve was to be his next pitch. He gripped the ball slightly off center and threw. The ball whistled toward the plate, then broke abruptly. "Great!" said Etchebarren. "Great slider!"

McNally tried it again. Another slider. He tried several. They all worked.

He could hardly believe it. When he had thrown the slider before, in 1962, he had held his wrist stiff. Now he was snapping his wrist and spinning the ball off his index finger.

The return of the pitch was of enormous value to McNally. Up until 1968 he had never won more than 13 games in a season. In 1968 he won 22; in 1969, 20; and in 1970, 24.

Few pitchers can develop both a good slider and a good curve. They must concentrate on one or the

SLIDER

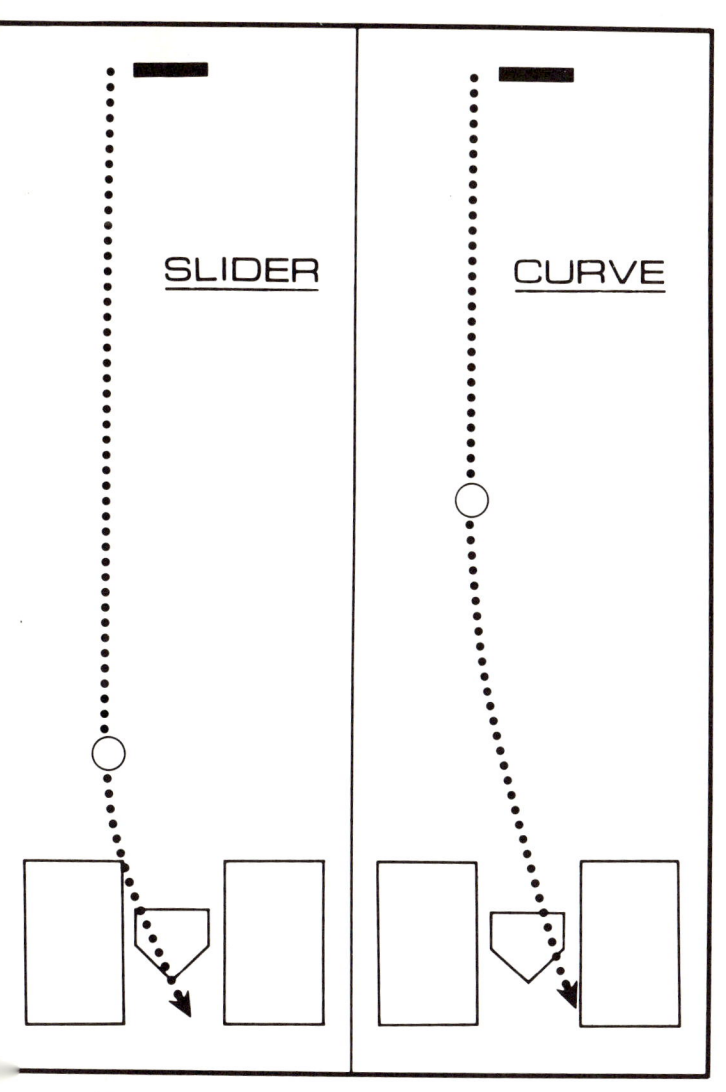

CURVE

other, although Dave McNally and Juan Marichal of the Giants are exceptions to the rule. Jerry Koosman, the Mets' curveball artist, was forbidden to throw the slider by the team's pitching coach, Rube Walker. Koosman didn't complain. "Taking away my slider gave better rotation to my curveball and made it more effective," he said.

Some mangers are less than enthusiastic about the slider. They feel that if a young man has a fastball, a curveball, and a change of pace, he shouldn't get involved with the slider. Their theory is that a pitcher should wait until his fastball begins to lose its zip before he starts working on the slider.

This chart, for a right-handed pitcher throwing to a right-handed batter, shows the difference between a curve and slider. The curve starts to break down and away at a point about 15 feet from the batter. The slider does not break until it is three or four feet from the batter.

THE SPECIALTY PITCHES

If pitchers threw only the standard pitches, things wouldn't be too difficult for hitters. But the fastball, curve, and slider are only part of the problem. There are also the specialty pitches.

THE KNUCKLE BALL

The term knuckle ball is something of a misnomer. "Fingernail ball" is more apt. What the knuckle-ball pitcher does is dig the nails of the index and middle fingers into the ball's cover. The thumb and little finger do the gripping. When he delivers, he snaps his wrist and straightens his fingers and "pushes" the ball toward the plate in a motion that is somewhat similar to putting the shot. The ball usually doesn't travel very fast, but the knuckle-ball pitcher isn't concerned about speed. What he wants is a ball that does not spin. When the knuckle ball is delivered right, the ball is so completely without motion that the batter can almost count the stitches.

Some knuckle-ball pitchers do use their knuckles. They grip the ball tightly with their thumb and fourth and little fingers, and bend their index and middle fingers so that the first joint of each comes in

Top: **The knuckle ball**
Bottom: **The knuckle ball; fingernail grip**

contact with the ball. The release is the same as described in the paragraph above.

The leading feature of the knuckler is that it arrives at the plate with its energy about expended and so is subject to the effects of air pressure or any capricious breeze that may be blowing. In other words, no one quite knows what the ball is going to do—not the pitcher, nor the catcher, and certainly not the batter. The ball may wobble toward the plate or float in. It may travel a path that's arrow-straight or dive crazily toward the ground. Or it may do all of these.

Knuckle-ball pitchers almost always work only in relief. But there is an exception—Phil Niekro of the Atlanta Braves. In 1969, a year the Braves won the Western Division championship in the National League, Niekro pitched 21 of the team's 38 complete games, four of their seven shutouts, and finished the season with a 23-13 record and billing as "the greatest knuckle-ball pitcher of all time."

Batters, however, were less than enthusiastic when speaking of Niekro. "He simply destroys you with that knuckle ball," said Ernie Banks of the Cubs. "It comes flying in there, dipping and hopping like crazy, and you just can't hit it."

Richie Allen, who starred with the Cardinals, Phillies, and Dodgers, was one of the few batters to

Phil Niekro is to the knuckler what Bob Feller was to the fastball.

Veteran Hoyt Wilhelm

claim that Niekro's knuckler didn't bother him. "I never worry about it," Allen said, following a game in which he struck out four times against it. "I just take my three swings and go and sit on the bench. I'm afraid if I even think about hitting it, I'll mess up my swing for life."

Hoyt Wilhelm was another pitcher of recent times who used the knuckle ball as his money pitch. It helped him to stretch his career—and stretch it and stretch it. Wilhelm began as a major leaguer with the New York Giants in 1952. In 1970, at the age of forty-six, he was still pitching. He made fifty appearances in relief for the Atlanta Braves and three for the Chicago Cubs that season.

Early in 1970, Wilhelm made his one-thousandth major league appearance. No other pitcher ever appeared in one thousand games. "If I had been a fastball pitcher, I wouldn't have lasted nearly so long," Wilhelm often said.

The Screwball

Many left-handed pitchers throw the screwball, or "screwjie," as it's sometimes called. Gripped like a fastball, and thrown like a curve, it breaks away from the right-handed batter. It's a reverse curve, in other words.

Right-handed pitchers have no need for such a pitch. They simply rely on conventional breaking pitches when facing right-handed batsmen.

Mike Cuellar of the Orioles mastered the art of the screwball better than any other pitcher of recent times. He threw the pitch at a variety of speeds, at least three of them, clipping the corners of the plate low and away and then down and in, and with a consistency that infuriated batters.

Coaches don't like to see young pitchers tinker with the screwball. It puts excessive strain on the elbow, and arm trouble can result.

THE FORKBALL

The forkball is held between the index and middle finger, sometimes with the middle finger along a seam. It is delivered overhand with a firm wrist snap.

Lindy McDaniel of the Yankees throws one of the best forkballs in the majors. Danny Frisella of the

Swivel-wristed Mike Cuellar has reason to grin. His screwball has been baffling hitters for years.

The forkball

Mets is another forkball specialist. Frisella hurt his arm throwing a slider and developed the forkball in its place. "When you grip the ball between your index and forefingers, you give the ball overspin," he says. "Throw it hard and it drops fast, just like a spitter."

THE SPITBALL

The spitball has been outlawed for more than fifty years, yet about 25 per cent of all pitchers use

Lindy McDaniel (left) is a leading practitioner of the forkball. Here he is pictured with New York pitching coach Jim Turner.

it and it's estimated that at least 90 per cent of all pitchers have tried it.

Saliva or other liquidy substance, when applied to the fingers that grip the ball along the seams, allows the pitcher to release the ball with a minimum of spin. The ball usually has some forward rotation and this imparts a tendency for the ball to break down, but overall its path to the plate is an erratic one, sort of a knuckler's flight—a damp knuckler, to be sure.

The spitball is no magical weapon—throw it and the batter misses. It's not like that at all. The spitball is the same as the fastball or curveball or any other pitch in that its quality varies. Some pitchers throw terrific spitballs, others are wholly inadequate with the pitch, and still others are in between.

The spitball was barred from the pitcher's repertoire in 1920. No official reason was given, although it is significant that the ban came not long after the infamous World Series of 1919 in which eight players of the favored Chicago Black Sox "sold out" to gamblers. Baseball, perhaps seeking to restore some luster to its faded image, barred the unwholesome spitball.

The prohibition is contained in Rule 8.02, which is as follows: "The pitcher shall not 1) apply a foreign substance of any kind to the ball; 2) expectorate either on the ball or in his glove; 3) rub the ball on his glove, person, or clothing; 4) deface the ball in any manner; 5) deliver what is called a 'shine' ball, 'spit' ball, 'mud' ball, or 'emery' ball.

"Penalty: For violation of any part of this rule the umpire shall immediately disqualify the pitcher, and the league president shall suspend the pitcher for a period of ten days."

The problem with the rule is that it is difficult—some say impossible—to enforce. The pitcher cannot dampen the surface of the ball, but how is an umpire to detect the dampening? The umpire sees the pitch coming and it breaks crazily. "A spitter!" the umpire thinks to himself, and he asks to examine the ball. The catcher reaches into his glove, digs out the ball, and hands it to him. By this time it's not damp any more.

It must be said at once that it doesn't take a great deal of spit to make the pitch work. Just a little dab will do. And it doesn't even require spit. Elwin (Preacher) Roe, a successful pitcher with the old Brooklyn Dodgers, admitted after his retirement that his source of supply was his sweaty forehead. Hair tonic is sometimes used. In the locker room before a game a pitcher will douse his head with "greasy kid stuff." Once on the mound he simply runs his fingers through his hair to "load up." A dollop of Vaseline on the outside of the pants leg is another ploy. By brushing his fingertips along his thigh the pitcher taps his supply.

Who throws the spitball? No one knows for sure because no pitcher will admit to committing the sin. After all, there's a ten-day suspension involved. But many pitchers are highly suspect.

Dean Chance, who was acquired by the Mets late in 1970, was thought to be a guilty party. An umpire once made Chance cleanse his hands with alcohol after an inspection showed a sticky substance on them. Gaylord Perry, a 23-game winner for San Francisco in 1970, wasn't always so effective. In 1965 he had an 8-12 record and an ERA of 4.18. The next season he won 21 games and his ERA dropped to 2.99. Batters said the transformation was the direct result of Perry's newly acquired spitter. Perry denied he threw the pitch. He said batters mistake his "super sinker" or "super slider" for the spitball. Bob Shaw of the Cubs and Phil Regan of the Dodgers were other pitchers said to indulge in spitball throws.

Gaylord Perry. Does he or doesn't he?

Baseball introduced legislation in 1968 which was meant to further limit the use of the spitter. The rule stated that the first time a pitcher brought his hand to his mouth he was to be warned by the umpire. The second time he did it he was to be ejected.

The rule was tried out during the exhibition season and about a dozen pitchers were banished from games. These men and all of their pitching colleagues screamed in protest. Putting one's hand to the mouth was a habit, a mere reflex action, many said. Others claimed they were simply blowing on a cold hand. The rule was moderated, with the penalty reduced from ejection to the mere calling of an illegal pitch, similar to calling a balk, an incomplete or misleading move toward the plate.

Many pitchers would like to see the ban lifted, to see the spitball legalized. But it's not likely to happen. "People come out to the ball parks to see hitting. The home run is baseball's most exciting moment," says one official. "We're not about to make things any easier for the pitchers. If anything, we're going to help the hitters."

The Palmball

A palmball is just what the name implies, a pitch that is held by the fingers plus the inner surface of

The palmball

the hand. Thrown with an overhand motion, the palmball has a tendency to behave like a sinker, to break downward.

The fingers, which are spread somewhat, grip the ball lightly. The thumb is positioned on the ball's underside. When released, the ball is allowed to slide from the thumb and fingers; there's little wrist action. The ball has a minimum amount of speed as a result.

Some pitchers use only a two-finger grip in delivering the palmball, but the ball is held well back in the hand, i.e., in the palm. The delivery is the same.

Of course, what makes a pitcher effective is not

Palmball specialist Dave Giusti

merely the ability to throw a sizzling fastball, a sharp-breaking screwball, or a bewildering knuckler. It's his skill with several pitches, plus his cleverness in mixing them up, that baffle the men at the plate. Juan Marichal of the San Francisco Giants, probably baseball's outstanding pitcher of the 1960's, has had a more puzzling variety of pitches than any other pitcher of recent times. Marichal used a fastball, slider, curve, and being a left-hander, a screwball. That's four pitches. But Marichal could throw each one either overhand or sidearm, which gave him a total of eight pitches. He had near perfect control of them all.

Because he threw so many pitches so well, many batters found Marichal to be the National League's toughest man to hit. "You cannot adjust to him," Orlando Cepeda once said. "When I go to the plate against him, I tell myself, 'Make up your mind to swing the bat. Don't wait. He's not going to give you anything good to hit.'"

The late Jack Zanger of *Sport* Magazine once asked Hank Aaron, "What's Marichal's best pitch?"

"He doesn't have any one best pitch," Aaron said, laughing. "Let's just say when he has to—or wants to—strike you out, he's got the pitch."

Juan Marichal, a pitching virtuoso

HOW THE BALL CURVES

After the curveball came into vogue late in the nineteenth century, a spirited controversy developed as to whether the ball actually curved or whether what it did was merely an optical illusion. The players, batters especially, swore that the ball really curved. Some scientists doubted it. The dispute continued for almost fifty years and even today it bubbles up every so often.

It is now accepted scientific fact that the ball does indeed curve. It is also true, however, that a certain amount of optical distortion is involved as well.

The first publicized test of what the curveball does was made in 1877. A. G. Spalding described the experiment in his book, *Baseball, America's National Game*. The test was made in Cincinnati before a large crowd. A surveyor set three posts in a row, twenty feet apart. Then two high fences were constructed, extending beyond each of the end posts and on a direct line with all three posts. Will White, a right-handed curveballer, stood to the left of the fence at one end of the layout. When he fired the ball, the fence prevented his hand from crossing the straight line between posts.

"White pitched the ball so that it passed to the right of the middle post," Spalding wrote. "This it did by three or four inches, but it passed the third post a half foot to the left."

Despite this convincing evidence, the controversy continued and eventually involved Igor Sikorsky, the noted aeronautical engineer. Sikorsky knew that a pitched ball which traveled in a curved path was an example of aerodynamic action, and the force that caused the curving was a manifestation of the "Magnus effect," first enunciated by Professor G. Magnus of Berlin in 1851.

Magnus' experiments dealt with the flight of cannon balls, but twenty-five years later a British physicist named Lord John Rayleigh applied Magnus' findings to the flight of a tennis ball. He concluded that when a ball is made to rotate sideways, friction between the ball and the air surrounding it caused differences in air pressure and resistance to build up on opposite sides of the ball.

The ball veers away from the side where the resistance is the greatest and toward the side where the resistance is the least. Since it keeps doing this over the entire distance of its flight, a curving path is the result. Gravity is what gives the ball's flight its downward slant.

This theory explains why the natural curve for a left-handed pitcher is toward the right. It's because he puts right-handed spin on the ball. This causes increased air resistance on the left side of the ball, so the ball veers to the right. In the case of a right-handed pitcher, the forces work in the opposite direction.

In conducting his experiment, Sikorsky first utilized rapid-fire flash photography to record how a

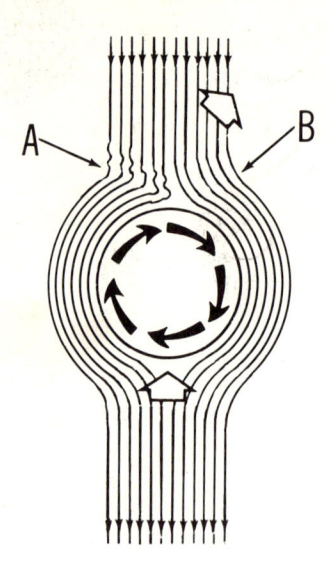

This diagram shows how a left-hander's curveball behaves in flight. It veers away from the side where the resistance is greatest (A), and toward the side where resistance is less (B).

pitch spun. His technicians examined the change in the ball's stitches from picture to picture and determined that the rate of spin was 600 revolutions per minute. Then they set up both an American League ball and a National League ball in a wind tunnel and rotated them.

Previous experiments had clocked Bob Feller's fastball at 98.6 miles per hour, so the Sikorsky engineers kept the air moving through the tunnel at speeds of from 80 to 100 miles an hour. The results, plotted on graph sheets, concluded that a pitched baseball actually does curve.

Dr. Lyman Briggs, former director of the National Bureau of Standards of the Department of Commerce, has added to what is known about the curveball. In his experiment, Dr. Briggs first attached a long strip of cloth tape to a baseball and had a pitcher use it to throw a curveball over the regulation distance. By counting the number of twists in the tape, Dr. Briggs calculated how many complete spins the baseball had made in its 60½-foot flight. Then, like Sikorsky, Dr. Briggs subjected the spinning ball to a measured force of air moving through a tunnel. He found that over the distance from the pitcher's hand to home plate, a ball could curve as much as 17½ inches from a straight line.

While baseball players and scientists agree that a ball actually does curve, there is still controversy as to the trajectory of the curve. Scientists say that every curve is a gradual curve. It begins when the ball leaves the pitcher's fingers and ends at the catcher's glove, and the angle is constant from start to finish. No pitcher, say the scientists, can make a ball curve abruptly just before it reaches home plate.

Hitters argue this point. They say that fastballs "move" or hop. They say that curveballs, sliders, and sinkers, and many other pitches break sharply just before they reach home plate. It was often said that Sandy Koufax's curveball had such a sudden downward break that it looked as if it had dropped off the end of a table.

Scientists contend this is an optical illusion. They explain it by pointing out that objects and movements appear smaller when they are farther away.

This dramatic photo, taken in a wind tunnel, reveals how a rising fastball acts in flight. Smoke filaments were spurted in from the right and the ball spun on a horizontal axis at right angles to the "wind." Notice the crowding together of the filaments over the top of the ball, an indication of decreased pressure. There is a corresponding increase in pressure toward the bottom of the ball. Together, these forces deflect the ball upward.
(Professor F. N. M. Brown, University of Notre Dame)

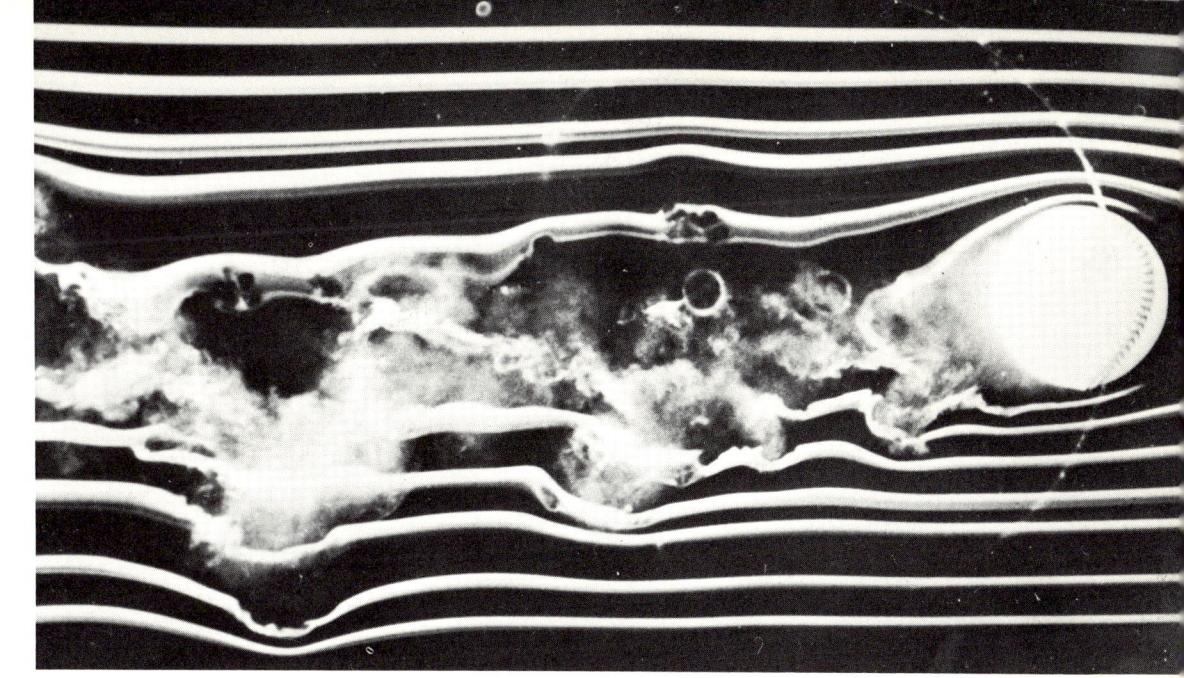

When the ball leaves the pitcher's hand, any change in direction appears slight, but when the ball is only a few inches away from the batter, the same amount of directional change appears much greater.

In other words, Sandy Koufax's curveball did not actually have an abrupt downward break just before it reached home plate. It only *seemed* to.

The next time you watch a baseball game on television, compare the amount of curveball break as seen by different cameras. A close-up camera—one behind home plate, for example—will show a pitcher's curveball to be breaking a great deal more sharply than a camera at a far distance from the pitcher—in center field, for instance. This is the same type of illusion that prevails when a batter says a pitcher's curveball breaks "just before home plate."

More than a few pitchers believe that they throw more effective curve balls on cool, dry days than they do when it is hot and humid. There's a scientific basis for this assumption.

On cool, dry days the air is heavier and more dense than on hot, humid days. The heavier the air, the more it resists a baseball moving through it, and the greater the differences in the air pressure around

Real break

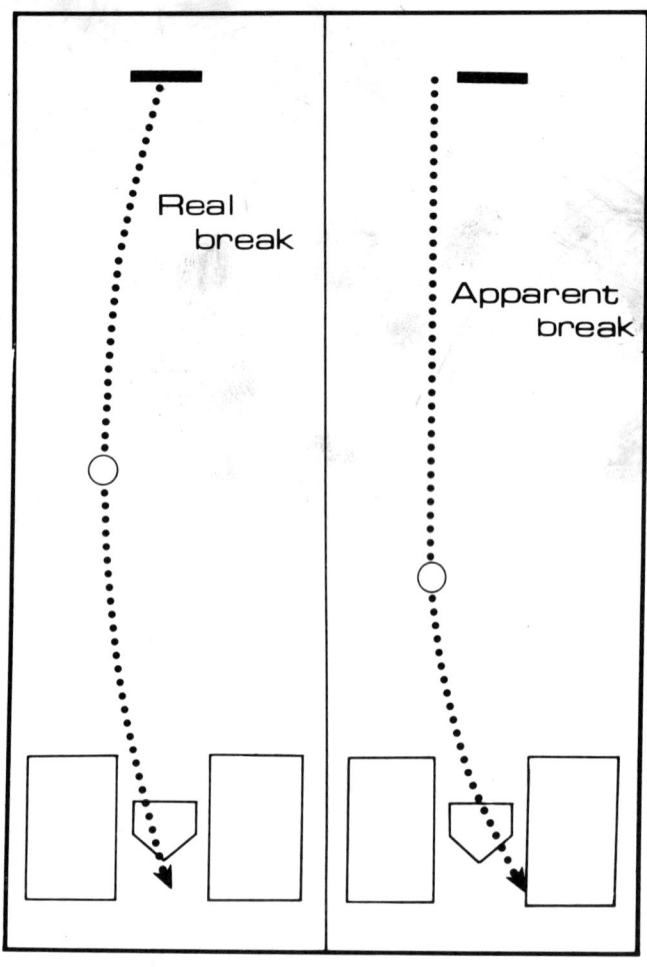

Apparent break

Scientists say that the curveball's break is as shown on the left in a rainbow pattern. The sharp break, as shown on the right, is an illusion.

Right: **Umbrellas (foreground) at Shea Stadium indicate that Jerry Koosman may have problems getting his curveball to break.**

the ball. This results in a curveball with a sharper break.

Altitude also affects the way a pitched ball behaves. In Denver, Colorado, which is about a mile above sea level, curveball pitchers have problems. The air is so thin that a pitched ball encounters little resistance. But fastballs travel with extra speed —again, because of the lack of air. Denver is no fastball pitcher's paradise, however. When struck by a bat, the ball travels extra distance, too.

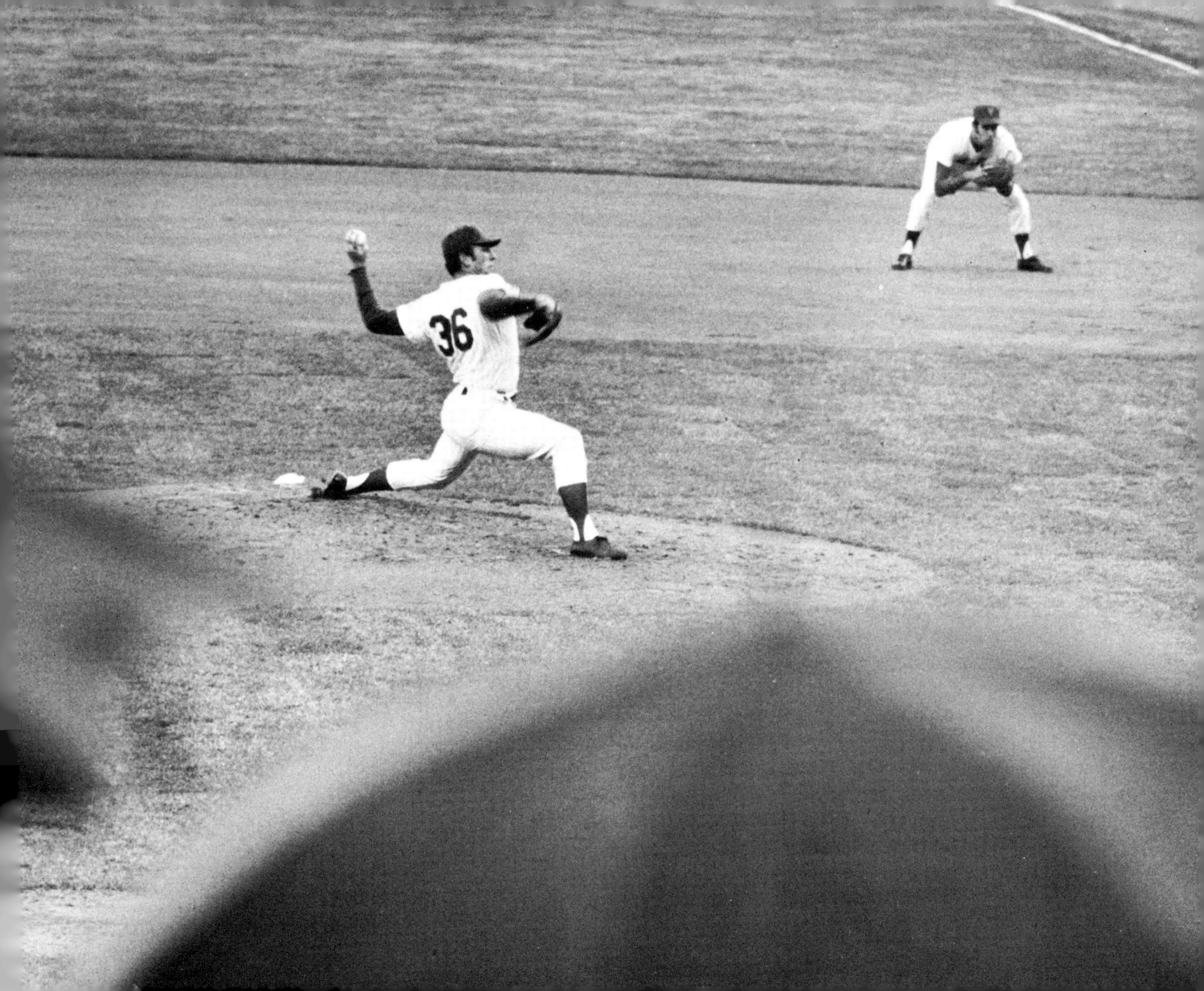

The Reds' Jim Merritt is one of baseball's top control pitchers.

CONTROL

Cincinnati ace Jim Merritt winds and delivers. The pitch nips the outside corner for strike one. Merritt winds again. It's low but on the inside corner and just at the batter's knees. Strike two. There's no waste pitch; Merritt comes right back with a breaking ball that catches the outside. The batter swings and pops to shortstop.

Control. That is Jim Merritt's style. By hitting the spots he became one of baseball's most successful pitchers.

Merritt has a fastball—a "decent" fastball, says Cincinnati catcher Johnny Bench—a curve, a slider he's not ashamed of, and a knuckler on occasions. But most of all he has the ability to graze the edges of the plate. When he's at his best, he can put only the seams over.

Being able to control the ball has always been vital to a pitcher's success, but it is even more important nowadays because the strike zone is smaller. Beginning with the 1969 season, the strike zone was defined as "the area from the armpit to the tip of the knee." Previously it had been "the area from the top of the shoulder to the bottom of the knee." It's width is the width of home plate—seventeen inches.

Control, however, is not merely a matter of getting the ball within the strike zone. That is not difficult for a major leaguer. Virtually every pitcher can put nine out of ten pitches within the strike zone without trying too hard. But a pitcher must have control *within* the strike zone. He must be able to target the ball on a very specific spot.

Suppose a right-handed pitcher is facing a right-handed batter. On the next pitch, he wants to get his fastball over the plate on the outside corner at the batter's knees. If he misses this spot to the outside or the pitch drifts low by as much as an inch, it is going to be called a ball. If he misses it to the inside or the ball rises, the pitch is likely to be drilled for a base hit. Accuracy is not enough; *deadly* accuracy is what is required.

Jim Merritt has this type of skill. "Most pitchers use my glove for a target," says Johnny Bench. "Not Merritt. He uses the pocket of my glove, and most of the time he hits it."

Tom Seaver's success with the New York Mets in recent years has been the result of many things: a fastball that is very fast, an assortment of good breaking pitches, his intelligence and desire. But his ability to control the ball is as much a factor as anything else. When Seaver is at his best, he says that he can throw a ball within a quarter of an inch of any spot on the plate nine times out of ten.

Nolan Ryan, a teammate of Seaver, threw a faster ball than Seaver, indeed, faster perhaps than anyone else in organized baseball, yet Ryan's advancement was retarded by his lack of control. Pitching coach Rube Walker said of him, "He gets wild in the strike zone, which is as bad as being wild and walking

Tom Seaver (right) is another control specialist. Here he is pictured with reliever Tug McGraw.

hitters. As fast as Nolan is, if he gives a man two or three good pitches in the strike zone to hit at, the chances are good that's just what the hitter will do."

Coaches say that young pitchers often experience control problems because they are too eager to get rid of the ball. They hurry in winding up and this disrupts their rhythm. Or a boy may be overly concerned with the technical aspects of his delivery and fail to concentrate on his target, the spot he's supposed to be pitching to.

Whatever the malady, a complete cure is necessary. Without control a man is never a complete pitcher; he's just a thrower.

A pitcher's mistake—Dave Roberts is a glum figure after serving a home-run ball to Ron Swoboda, who rounds third base.

PITCHING STRATEGY

The pitcher's goal is clear-cut: to make the batter swing and miss, or to make him take a called strike, or to prevent him from hitting the ball solidly. To achieve one of these alternatives, the pitcher relies on a body of strategy with as many aspects as a large-scale military operation, and often it is administered with the same belligerence.

The basis of the pitcher's tactical strength is his ability to "mix his pitches." He varies not only the kind of pitches he throws, going from fastball to curve to change-up, and so on, but also varies the character of each—that is, the speed, the degree of break, and the point to which the ball is thrown, high or low, inside or outside.

There are many factors that influence the pitcher's decision as to which pitch is precisely the "right" pitch in a given situation. The count is important. A pitcher doesn't deliver the same pitch when the count is no balls, two strikes as he does when the count is two balls, no strikes. When he is behind a hitter—when the count is in the hitter's favor—he may forget strategy, and simply put all his effort into getting the ball over the plate.

The number of outs—the score—and whether there are men on bases, and, if so, what bases, are also important in deciding the right pitch. Suppose it is the ninth inning of a game between the Yankees and the Orioles. One man is out and a runner is on third. The score is tied. Fritz Peterson is facing Paul Blair. Twice the Yankee pitcher has gotten Blair to overswing at fastballs, and harmless fly balls have been the result. But with the tie-breaking run on third base, Peterson has to formulate new strategy.

The pitch he normally uses to get Blair is no longer the right pitch.

The prevailing weather conditions and even the time of day have an effect, too. Is there a wind? Is it blowing in or out, to the right or left? Where is the sun? Is the batter standing in a shaded area? These are a few of the questions a pitcher must ask—and answer.

If the count favors the pitcher, he may decide to "waste" or "show" a pitch. In execution these are much the same, but there is a sharp difference in what each is meant to accomplish.

The waste pitch is a "bad" pitch, one that is outside of the strike zone, but it is thrown to an area that is known to be enticing to the batter. Even if the batter connects with the pitch, he is not going to hit it solidly or for any distance.

When a pitcher "shows" a pitch, he also delivers it outside the strike zone, but his intent is not the same. Suppose a pitcher is facing a batter who is well known for his ability to hit "off-speed" pitches, i.e., the change of pace. The count is one strike and no balls. Now is a good time to show the batter the change-up. When the pitcher delivers, he keeps the ball out of the strike zone. If the batter swings, he's going to hit a bad ball, but the pitcher really doesn't intend for him to swing. The idea of the off-speed pitch is to upset the batter's timing, to set him up for the next pitch. Following the change of pace, the pitcher is going to come through with a fastball or a fast curve. In contrast to the previous pitch, it looks even faster.

A curve is often thrown "off," or following, a fastball. The speed of the curve is less; it's path is different. It's these contrasts that make it difficult to hit.

What pitch a man decides to show may depend on the relative effectiveness of the pitches in his repertoire. After warming up, a pitcher may say to his catcher, "I'm having trouble controlling the slider today. Let's just show them the slider and try to get them out with the curve."

When a pitcher does intentionally miss with a pitch, he is careful to miss in the right direction. Suppose Mel Stottlemyre it pitching to Boog Powell. Most pitchers try to break the ball in toward Powell's hands, to "jam" him. When Stottlemyre seeks to do this, he makes sure that if the ball is going to miss the plate, it misses inside. If the ball misses the other way by just an inch or two, Powell has the quickness and strength to smash it out of the park.

This type of tactical planning and execution is necessary on every pitch. There cannot be even a momentary lapse. Batters don't hit good pitching. It's pitchers' mistakes that boost batting averages and inflate home-run totals.

Pitching strategy also includes "brushback" and "knockdown" pitches. Indeed, they are as much a part of baseball as Sunday double-headers.

Players have several different expressions to describe the act of throwing high and close to a batter.

Jerry Koosman reacts to a high, tight pitch.

The manager, in speaking about the man at the plate, may tell the pitcher to "Loosen him up" or "Keep him honest" or "Spin his cap."

"Let's hear a little chin music out there," is another expression. "Chin music" refers to throwing near the chin.

The brushback is used to move back a batter who is crowding the plate, an act the pitcher regards as a trespass. A batter who is crowding the plate is in a position to hit outside pitches. The brushback sends him back where he belongs.

Pitchers also use the brushback to regain respect. A batter who consistently hurts a pitcher with his hitting is not being respectful; he is intimidating the pitcher. A fastball under the bill of the cap restores the balance.

The first time an umpire suspects a pitcher of throwing at a batter he is warned that if he does it again he will be ejected. If the pitcher persists, he not only is immediately ejected but he becomes liable for a fine and suspension. However, these penalties have not served to curb the brushback to any degree.

Don Drysdale, who won over 200 games with the Dodgers during the late 1950's and 1960's, owed much of his success to his aggressiveness, his willingness to throw high and inside without the slightest hesitation. Drysdale hit more batters than any other pitcher in National League history, 154 of them. Bill Singer, a Dodger star of the 1970's, was said to follow in the Drysdale tradition. But Singer is no exception. Every front-line pitcher will fire the brushback whenever occasion demands.

While brushing back a batter is not at all unusual, throwing at a man to hit him is more of a rarity—yet it happens. A teammate of the pitcher may have been hit with a pitch in an earlier inning. Or perhaps there was a play at second base in which the enemy baserunner took unfair advantage of the shortstop or second baseman. It's at times like these that the pitcher may attempt to nick the man at the plate. In other words, it's a means of retaliation.

In a game against the Chicago Cubs not long ago, Tom Seaver pitched high and very tight to Ron Santo. When Seaver came to the plate in the next inning, Chicago pitcher Bill Hands hit Seaver on the forearm.

That was not the end of it. When Hands came to bat, a Seaver pitch struck *him* on the left leg.

In the clubhouse afterward, Seaver was asked to explain the fireworks. Seaver shrugged. "Baseball," he said, "is a tough game."

The Dodgers' Bill Singer is known for his "aggressiveness."

THE BOOK

If you pitched in the National League in 1971, you'd know enough to pitch a strike to Roberto Clemente on the first pitch (because he was likely to take it), throw high and inside to Ernie Banks (so he couldn't get around on the ball), and fire low-and-away curves to Tommy Agee (getting him to lunge for the ball).

Information of this type is derived from the "book" on each batter, from the elaborately detailed body of intelligence that reveals hitters' strengths and weaknesses. The book on the tough hitters in the line-up of the Baltimore Orioles in 1970, the year the team won the World Series, read like this:

Paul Blair—A fastball hitter who overswings. Keep the ball away from him. Throw him curves.

Frank Robinson—Has enough power to hit the ball out of the park in any direction, but has a tendency to try and pull. Keep the ball outside. Throw breaking pitches.

Boog Powell—Tremendously strong. Aggressive at the plate. Can be pitched to. Throw breaking pitches. Gets his hands over the plate. Jam him.

Brooks Robinson—Fine clutch hitter. A good breaking-ball hitter. Jam him.

Elrod Hendricks—Erratic. Keep the ball high and tight.

Mark Belanger—Hits the ball where it's pitched. Doesn't strike out often. Jam him.

Before a team begins a series, its pitchers meet in the clubhouse with the coaches and manager and discuss the opposition line-up, hitter by hitter. A coach may tell a pitcher he can get Tony Conigliaro out with a curve inside and low. Then the pitcher has to ask himself, "Is he talking about *my* curveball? How will Conigliaro react to *it*?"

In his book, *Ball Four*, Jim Bouton recalled a

Pitchers try to take advantage of the fact that Frank Robinson often tries to pull the ball.

The book on Harmon Killebrew: "No weaknesses"

meeting between pitchers and coaches when Tim McCarver, then with the Cards, was being discussed. Sandy Koufax gets McCarver out on letter-high fastballs, one coach said. Bouton declared that was "great advice"—if you happened to throw chest-high fastballs the way Koufax did.

Much of what a team knows about the opposition is derived from the pitching chart, an extremely detailed sheet that is maintained during each game by the pitcher who is to work the next day. For each pitch delivered that day by his teammate—or mates, if relief pitchers are called in—this information is recorded:

• The type of pitch thrown (fastball, curve, change-up, etc.).
• Where the pitch was thrown (the area—high or low, outside or inside).
• What resulted (a ball, called strike, or swinging strike; or, if the ball was hit, where it was hit).

The chart tells many things about the batters. It

SYMBOLS

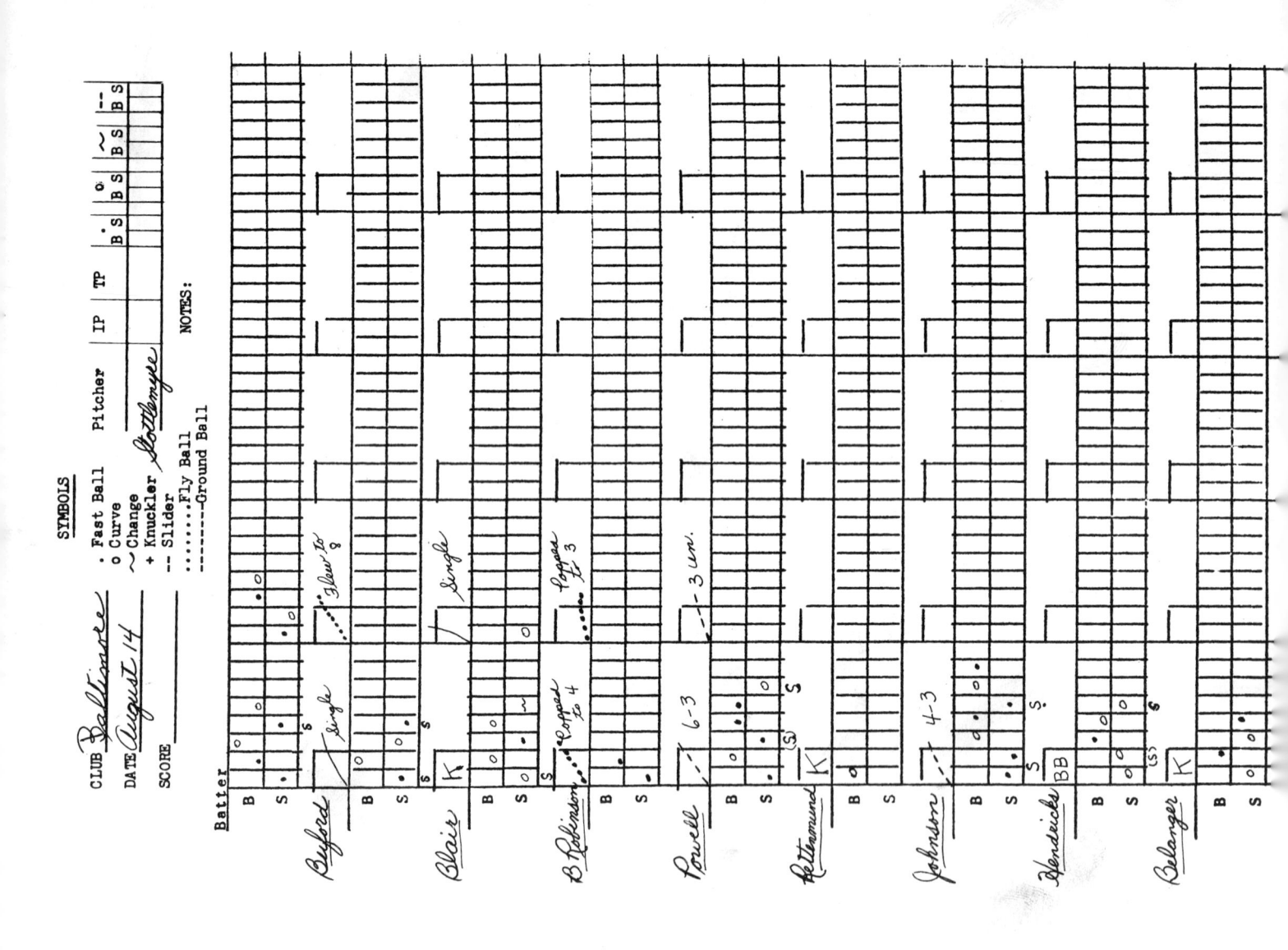

- . Fast Ball
- o Curve
- ~ Change
- + Knuckler
- -- Slider
- ...... Fly Ball
- ------ Ground Ball

CLUB *Baltimore*
DATE *August 14*
SCORE _____

Pitcher *Stottlemyre*

NOTES:

This is a pitching chart, the type used by the New York Yankees. It details what happened in the first three innings of a game against the Baltimore Orioles. Other teams use charts that are similar.

The chart contains spaces to record the results of five at-bats for each opposition player. In this example, Yankee pitcher Mel Stottlemyre faced four batters in the first inning, four in the second, and five in the third, a total of thirteen batters.

Notice the double row of small rectangular boxes within each one of the larger at-bat boxes. One row is labled S, for strikes, and the other B, for balls. The small symbols with these boxes indicate to what area of the strike zone each pitch (fastball, curve, or change-up) was delivered. When a small S is entered under one of these boxes, it indicates the strike was a swinging strike. A small dot under the S signifies a foul ball. When the S is enclosed in parentheses, it indicates the pitch was outside the strike zone.

A large K means a strikeout. When the K is in reverse, it indicates a called third strike. Other symbols used are the same as those employed in keeping a conventional baseball scorebook.

In the first inning of this game, Don Buford worked the count to three-and-two, and then singled on the ground between first and second. Paul Blair struck out swinging. Brooks Robinson popped out to the second baseman. Boog Powell grounded out, shortstop to first base.

In the second inning, Merv Rettenmund struck out. Dave Johnson ground out, second to first. After a base on balls to Ellie Hendricks, Mark Belanger struck out.

Jim Palmer struck out to begin the third inning. Then Buford lifted a fly ball to center field. Blair followed with a single through the hole between shortstop and third base. Robinson popped to the third baseman. Powell grounded out to the first baseman, who made the play unassisted.

reveals who is swinging at what pitches. It discloses what kind of pitches are effective with particular batters. And what ones are not.

The chart also gives revealing information about the pitcher. It tells how many pitches he is throwing and discloses his ball and strike ratio. It helps the manager find out if a pitcher is falling into any careless habits. He may, for example, be throwing a fastball as every first pitch of the inning. If the opposition comes to realize this, it can hurt.

Baseball usually has two or three hitters who have no real weaknesses, and have such enormous physical strength that they can hit virtually any pitch, even a "bad" pitch, for distance. Harmon Killebrew of the Minnesota Twins is one such slugger. The fact that he has struck over 500 home runs in his major league career is evidence of this. One year he was granted 145 bases on balls, a statistic which testifies to the cautionary attitude pitchers have toward him.

Gary Peters of the White Sox once threw Killebrew a sinker low and away, the type of pitch which, if it is hit, is almost certain to be a ground ball. Killebrew hit it over the fence. "It was the best pitch I've ever thrown for a home run," Peters recalls sadly.

Most pitchers agree that at one time Killebrew had a weakness and could be pitched to. In his early years, he had a tendency to go after bad-breaking pitches, but as he gained experience he repaired this chink in his armor.

A pitcher like Sam McDowell, who had one of the game's fastest fastballs, could sometimes overpower Killebrew with his speed. But pitchers of McDowell's eminence are as rare as catchers who hit .300. For every single one of the American League's pitchers, Killebrew is a burning problem.

Some observers say his greatest asset, besides his strength, is his ability to wait—to wait until the very last instant before bringing the bat around. "Keep mixing up your pitches. Keep moving the ball. That's about all you can do when he comes to the plate," says one pitcher.

A reporter once asked Mel Stottlemyre of the New York Yankees how he pitched to Killebrew. Stottlemyre thought for a while, then said, "Carefully, very carefully."

RELIEF PITCHING

Dave Giusti, a stocky right-hander for the Pittsburgh Pirates, is the team's leader. "He's always thinking of how to beat the other guy," says Danny Murtaugh, the Pittsburgh manager. "He believes his job begins when he gets to the clubhouse, not when it's time for him to start warming up."

Giusti is extremely knowledgeable and an intense competitor. He usually has the best earned run average on the Pirate staff. He is one of the leaders in the salary department, too.

It also happens that Giusti is a relief pitcher, one of the "new wave" of relievers. A decade or so ago, men who followed Giusti's trade seldom achieved eminence. It used to be that a reliever was merely a pitcher not good enough or not experienced enough to be a starter. But that system has gone the way of the crew haircut. Today's relievers are absolute masters of the art of pitching well and frequently for short periods of time. Sometimes, as in Dave Giusti's case, they are the best pitchers a team has.

Giusti, who is noted for his palmball, warms up anytime the game is close, even if it means getting loose three or four days in succession. Sometimes he makes four or five relief appearances in a week.

At one time Giusti's goal was to be a starting pitcher. Though he hasn't realized his ambition, Giusti has no complaints. "No longer is the relief

The Pirates' Dave Giusti

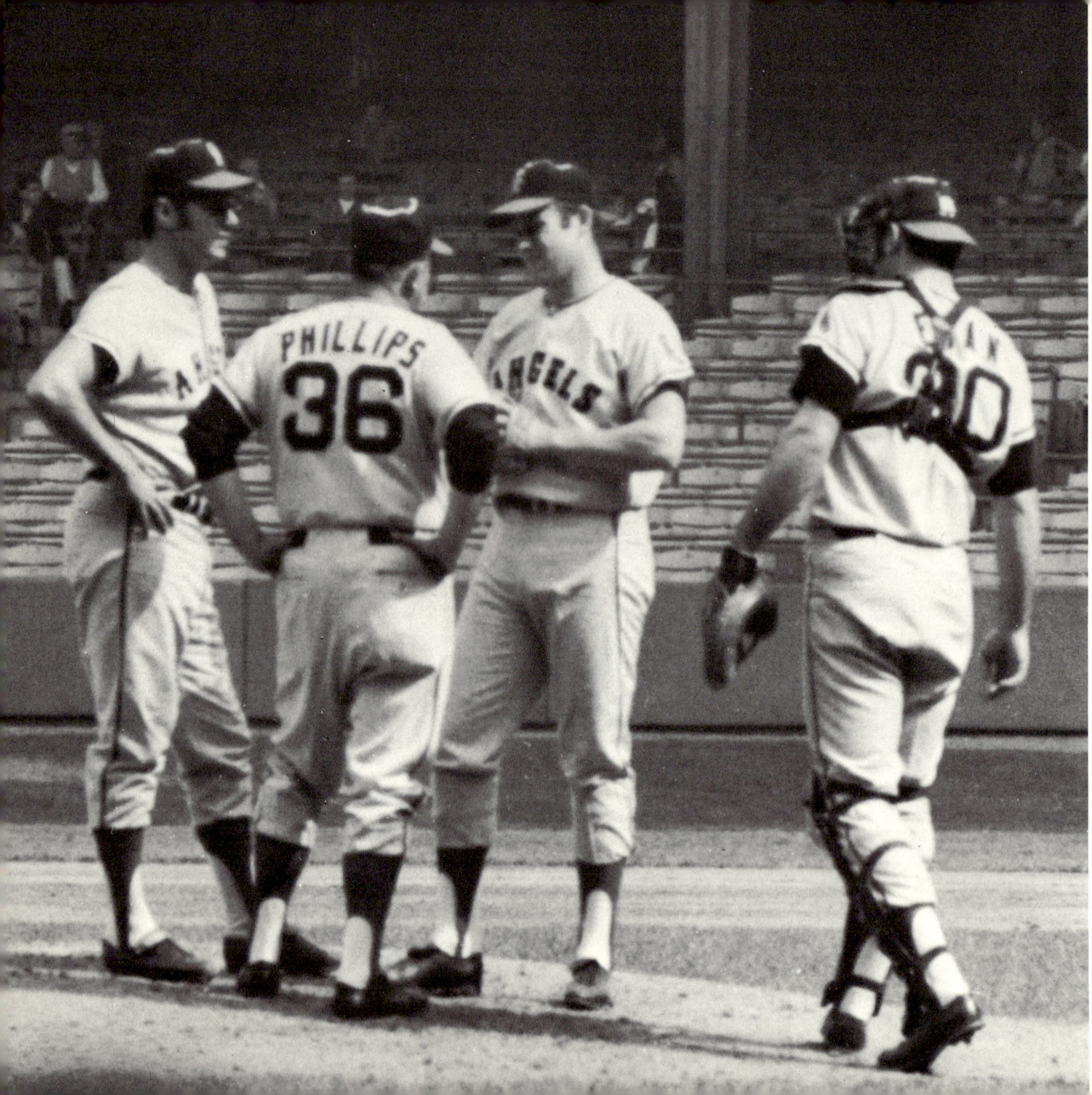
PHILLIPS
36
ANGELS

Manager Lefty Phillips of the Angels tells Andy Messersmith to take an early shower.

man just a 'throw-in,' " he says. "If he can produce, he's rewarded."

Most teams carry four or five relief specialists. At least two of these are "long men," relievers who are meant to pitch five, six, or more innings. The "short" relievers work only an inning or two, or maybe only a portion of an inning, but they may see action fifty or sixty times a year.

The short relief man has to have one outstanding pitch. It can be an overpowering fastball, a bewildering knuckler, a palmball, a forkball—anything. He has to have other pitches, too, but one that is virtually unhittable is a must.

His job is to come into the game in the eighth inning, say, pitch the balance of the inning and perhaps all of the ninth. If he does his job well, he will pitch to only five or six batters. One superior pitch is sufficient to accomplish his task. He could not be expected to start a game and go the full distance because batters would get accustomed to seeing his specialty and start mauling it. But in his brief term on the mound, no hitter sees him more than once.

He also has to be the type of person who is not easily ruffled. Anytime he's called upon to pitch, there's trouble. The sirens are wailing. Enemy runners are on the bases, a tough pinch hitter is at the

The quality of patience is a must for relief pitchers. This is the Mets' Tug McGraw.

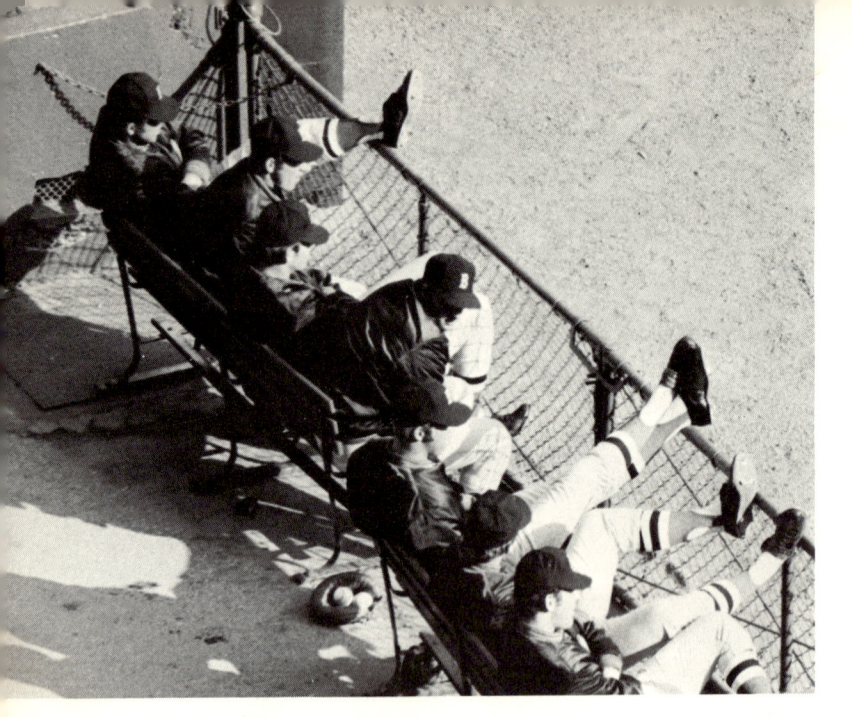

Red Sox relievers watch the action at Yankee Stadium.

Lindy McDaniel of the Yankees led all relief pitchers in 1970 with a 2.01 ERA.

plate, and the fans are likely to be screaming. But the pitcher has to remain as cool as an arctic breeze.

His arm has to have a certain quality to it, a rubberiness. He has to be capable of warming up quickly and often, perhaps several times a week.

One other quality is important: patience, the patience to endure the wearisome hours in the bullpen.

Why is it called the "bullpen?" There are two explanations. One is that in days gone by pitchers awaiting the call to action would pass away the time by chewing tobacco, and one of the most popular brands was Bull Durham. The other explanation is probably the more valid. The favorite activity of all bullpen regulars is "shooting the bull."

A telephone links the bullpen and the dugout. When trouble looms, the manager or pitching coach calls the bullpen coach and tells him who should start warming up.

The manager's decision as to whether or not to bring in a relief man is based on several factors—the game situation (the inning, the score, the number of outs) and the upcoming batter (his over-all skill, his showing in the game, whether he bats right-handed or left-handed). But an overriding consideration is who's available for relief. If the manager has a reliable pitcher ready, then there is a much greater likelihood the man on the mound will be lifted.

The manager makes up his mind before he leaves the dugout. What a pitcher has to say when the manager reaches the mound seldom influences the decision.

Relief pitchers, like starters, are rated on the basis of their earned run averages. A good relief pitcher is one whose ERA is between 2.00 and 2.75. Lindy McDaniel of the Yankees led all relief pitchers in 1970 with a 2.01 ERA.

A relief pitcher receives credit for a win if he is the pitcher of record (the pitcher who possibly may be the winning or losing pitcher) at the time his

Ron Perranoski represents the "new wave" of relief specialists.

team assumes the lead. However, there are exceptions. If he is the pitcher of record when his team goes ahead, but is ineffective in his relief stint, the succeeding pitcher is likely to be awarded the win.

The starting pitcher has to complete at least five innings in order to be credited with a win. If the starting pitcher leaves the game before the beginning of the sixth inning, and his team is ahead and stays ahead, the win goes to the relief pitcher judged to be the more effective by the official scorer.

A relief pitcher can also win a "save." He earns a save anytime he enters a game with his team in the lead and holds the lead for the remainder of the game (provided he is not credited with a victory). He must finish the game to be credited with the save (unless he is removed for a pinch-hitter or pinch runner).

Under these provisions, it sometimes happens that more than one relief pitcher qualifies for a save. In this case, the relief pitcher judged by the official scorer to be the most effective receives credit for the save.

The Sporting News rates relief pitchers by means of a point system, giving a man one point for winning a game in relief and another point for every save he earns. At the end of the season, the pitcher with the highest point total in each league receives the "Fireman of the Year" trophy. Wayne Granger of the Reds and Ron Perranoski of the Twins won the award in 1970. Granger had 29 points (23 saves and 6 wins); Perranoski had 41 points (34 and 7). The two also won the award in 1969 and rank as the only repeat winners. They, like Dave Giusti, typify the relief specialist of the 1970's.

CATCHERS

Catchers, and their wives, too, are quick to point out that the pitcher represents only one-half of the two-man unit known as the battery. The catcher is the other half.

While, granted, the catcher is physically one-half of this two-man combination, his importance to it varies. When a rookie pitcher is throwing to a veteran catcher, it is the catcher who decides what pitches the man on the mound should fire. But in the case of an experienced pitcher, it's he who "calls the game." He may not actually signal every pitch—in fact, he may not signal any at all—but the two men work in such close harmony that they think as one, and the catcher's signals are merely a confirmation of what the pitcher wants to throw.

Many different pitcher-catcher combinations use the same signals: one finger for a fastball; two fingers for a curve, and three fingers for a slider.

In order to prevent one of the opposing coaches or a runner on first or third from seeing the signal, the catcher puts his hand on the inside of his right thigh when crouching and holds his mitt alongside his left knee, thus screening his fingers and their coded message.

Some teams use a "pump" system of signaling. In this, the number of fingers is not the important thing, it's how many times the fingers are flashed or "pumped." One pump may be a fastball, two a curve, and three a slider.

If a team feels that the opposition is stealing its signs, the pitcher and catcher can use an "indicator" in combination with the pump. It works like this: The pitches are numbered in sequence. Let's say that one finger is the fastball, two the curve, three the change-up, and four the slider. Before an inning begins, the pitcher and catcher decide on the indicator number they are going to use. Say it is three. This means the sequence begins with the No. 3 pitch. So, in the example above, one pump would be the change-up, two the slider, three the fastball, and four the curve. Simply by changing the indicator number, the coded signals for all the pitches are changed.

The indicator can also take the form of another type of signal that the catcher flashes. Touching the inside of the right thigh with his right hand, for instance. With this as an indicator, the catcher may flash a series of several finger signals, but the only valid signal is the one that is flashed after he touches his thigh. The real sign can be flashed immediately after the indicator, or it can be the second sign given after the indicator, or the third, or whatever number the catcher and pitcher decide upon.

When the opposition has a runner on second base, the man there can see the catcher's signals almost as plainly as the pitcher. Occasionally this can cause difficulty. The late Charlie Dressen, a major league coach and manager for more than two decades, instructed baserunners who reached second to tell him what signs were being used. Then Dressen would compare this intelligence with the actual pitches and seek to break the code. When the next runner reached second, he would signal the batters as to the upcoming pitch. He'd do it with his feet. If the runner used his right foot as his lead-off foot, it meant a fastball was coming. A left-foot lead meant a breaking pitch.

From time to time, stories crop up about teams that post a binocular-equipped player in the bullpen, the bleachers, the center-field stands, or even within the scoreboard, and whose task it is to pick up the catcher's signs. Once the spy establishes a pattern between the signals and what the pitcher is throwing, he starts flashing the upcoming pitches to the batter.

All such plotting is usually not worth the effort. As was pointed out, the pitcher and catcher can change signs with the greatest of ease and often do. There's another reason the amount of sign stealing is minimal. Suppose you are the batter and an agent posted in center field informs you that a curve is on the way. But the information is dead wrong. The pitcher and catcher, aware that something is awry, have reversed signs. A fastball is coming in. You take a lusty swing—and miss it by a foot and a half. What is even worse is to be told a fastball is on its

Pitcher and catcher must think as one. Here Bob Gibson and Joe Torre discuss strategy.

way and have the pitcher blaze in a sharp curve. You'd better be wearing a quality batting helmet.

Sometimes a pitcher will shake off a catcher's sign. He will simply shake his head "no" or he'll flick his glove. One flick may mean he wants to add one number to the signal—change a two to a three, for example. Two flicks may mean he wants to add two numbers.

Shaking off the catcher's signal is something of a rarity nowadays, and much of the head-shaking and glove-flicking the fan observes is meant to confuse the batter. "I can signal for pitches 110 times in a game," says catcher Jerry Grote of the Mets, "and the only time Tom Seaver shakes me off is when we plan it that way to make the hitter think we're guessing. But it's the hitter who's doing the guessing."

The rapport between catcher and pitcher breaks down occasionally, and when it does it usually produces unhappy results—unhappy for the pitcher, that is. A game between the Atlanta Braves and New York Mets late in 1970 is a case in point. The Mets were ahead, 2-1, in the ninth inning. Tom Seaver was the pitcher for the Mets. The Braves filled the bases. Bob Tillman came to bat.

Earlier in the game Seaver had struck out Tillman on a curve, which had followed an array of sliders and fastballs. This time the count reached one ball and two strikes and Jerry Grote signaled for a curve. But Seaver had decided a fastball would do the trick. He failed to inform Grote, however.

The runners led off as Seaver went into his wind-up. The ball came blazing in. Tillman, looking for a curve, let the ball go by. Grote shifted to his right to handle the pitch as it broke. Of course, it never did any breaking. It sailed over Grote's left shoulder, caromed off the plate umpire's mask, and bounced all the way to the screen. By the time Grote recovered the ball, the tieing and winning runs were across the plate.

Occasionally a catcher comes along with exceptional skills and a "command personality," and it is he who will be the dominant figure in the pitcher-catcher relationship. Johnny Bench, who was Rookie Player of the Year for the Cincinnati Reds in 1968 and the National League's Most Valuable Player in 1970, is one such catcher.

Even as a twenty-year-old rookie, Bench sometimes dominated older and more experienced pitchers. In one game, Bench demanded that veteran pitcher Jim Maloney throw a change-up curve to a batter to get a third strike. Maloney, who owned one of the best fastballs in the game, promptly shook him off. Bench again demanded the slow curve. Maloney, now visibly upset, shook it off. "Who does this kid think he is?" Maloney was thinking. But Bench would not back down. He signaled the curveball a third time. Not wishing to continue the standoff, Maloney came in with the slow curve. "Strike!" bellowed the umpire, ending the inning.

Back in the dugout, Maloney glared at Bench.

"Well," he said, "you got away with it—this time."

"The guy froze," said Bench. "He was so surprised he didn't even move."

Maloney was silent for a moment, then said softly, "I noticed."

Bench watches batters carefully for tip-offs as to what pitch to call. If he sees a power hitter open his stance, an indication he's going for distance, Bench is likely to signal the pitcher to jam the man with a fastball close to the hands. If he sees a batter adjust his feet slightly, to suggest that he is looking for a curve, Bench will give the fastball sign.

Bench draws upon a rich store of knowledge he has acquired about each batter's likes and dislikes. He has been collecting information about ballplayers since he was twelve, when he used to sit by the family television set and jot down in notebooks what players said during interviews.

Born in Oklahoma City on December 7, 1947, Bench spent a good part of his childhood competing with two older brothers. His father, who had been a semipro catcher, gave him rigorous training in baseball. He would station someone a hundred or so feet in back of second base and have Johnny practice the catcher's throw from behind home plate. When it came to catching in a game, the throwing distance from home plate to second base, about 127 feet, was a cinch for him, and he could throw the ball arrow-straight.

Johnny was a good student in high school and

Johnny Bench, the Reds' supercatcher

Opposite: Bench squats low as he awaits the pitch. Art Shamsky is the batter.

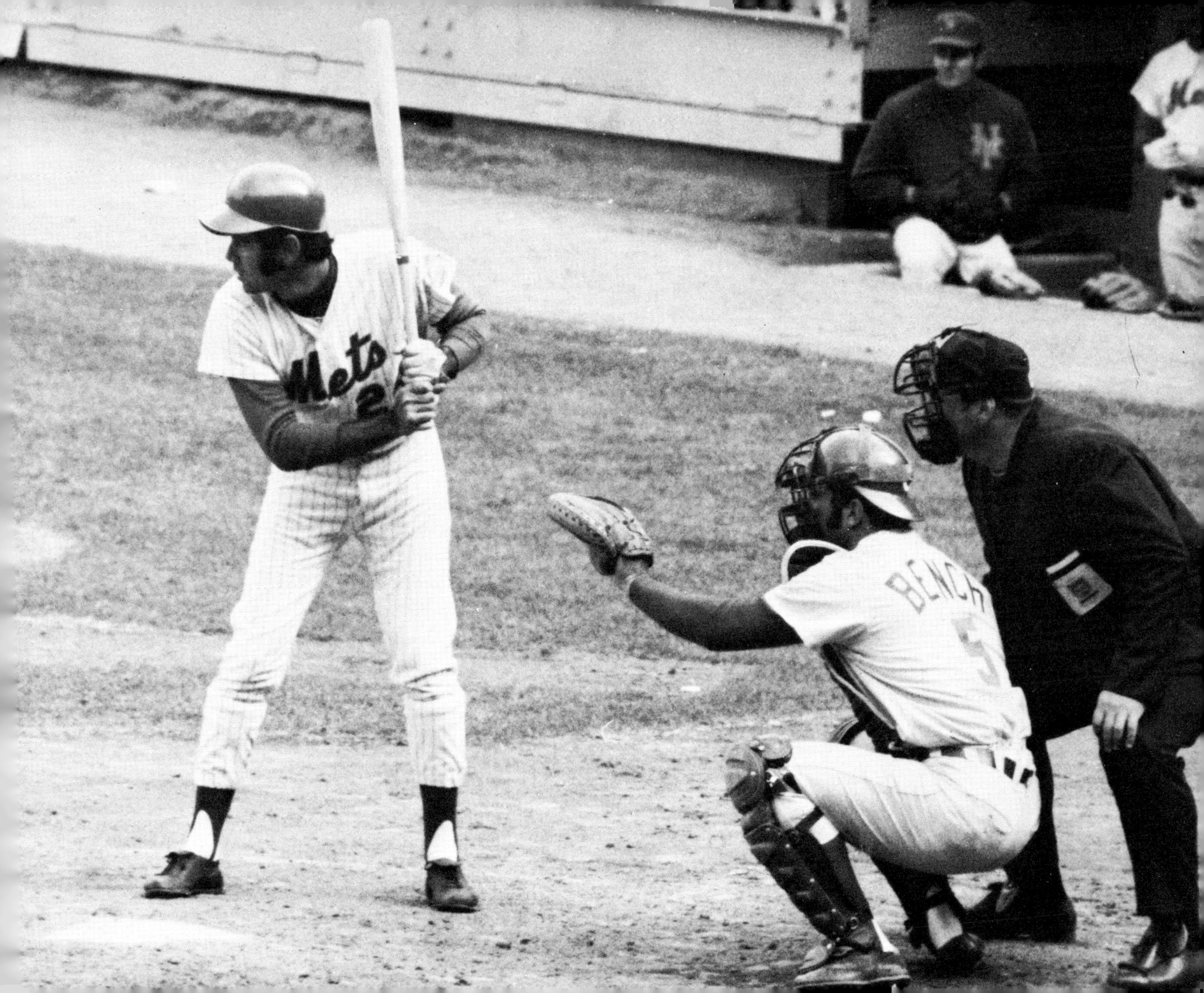
Mets
BENCH

graduated first in his class. Instead of going to college, he accepted a bonus offer of about $10,000 from the Cincinnati Reds following an American Legion baseball tournament in 1965. After three years of minor league seasoning, he joined the Reds as a regular.

Besides being a master strategist, Bench can hit, field, and pick off baserunners. Baseball men say that he plays the game in a manner reminiscent of Mickey Cochrane, Bill Dickey, and Roy Campanella, catching's all-time greats.

Sometimes Bench goads a pitcher into being effective. Early in his career, Bench was once catching reliever Gerry Arrigo in a game against the Dodgers. Arrigo liked to throw slow stuff and even his fastball lacked real zip. This upset Bench. When he called for a fastball, he wanted the ball to hum, not come in soft. He went to the mound repeatedly to speak to Arrigo, but the pitcher persisted. Bench went to the mound one more time. He spoke to the pitcher heatedly, then returned to the plate. He set his mitt as a target and waited. Arrigo took a windmill windup and once more he floated the ball in.

The pitch was slightly outside. Bench leaned to his right, stuck up his bare hand and made the catch. Then, without moving out of his crouch, he snapped the ball back to Arrigo harder than the pitcher had thrown it in. The players in both dugouts stared in openmouthed amazement. Arrigo got the message. His next pitch was a genuine fastball.

Bench is of good size—6-foot-1, almost 200 pounds—so he gives the pitcher a wide target. And he squats down lower than almost every catcher in the league. Keeping the ball low is vital, of course.

There are subtle ways Bench helps, too. Suppose there is a runner on first base. Many catchers prefer that the succeeding pitches come in fast and high and outside. That's the kind of a pitch that is easiest to catch and the easiest to convert into a throw. The catcher merely has to cock his arm.

But the hard, high pitch is the easiest to hit, and so pitchers are reluctant to throw it. A pitcher prefers to keep the ball low and inside anytime there's a runner on base. This is a continual conflict, and the failure to resolve it has cost countless ball games.

With Bench there is no such struggle. He can handle a low inside curve or an outside fastball with just about the same alacrity. So if the curve happens to be the right pitch with runners on base, Bench won't hesitate to call it.

Catchers like Johnny Bench are almost as rare as .400 hitters. Seldom does the man behind the plate hold sway over the man on the mound. Normally, it is the other way around.

THE PITCHING COACH

The pitching coach plays a vital role in a pitcher's life, perhaps even a more important one than that of his manager. No pitcher receives an assignment of any kind without a discussion between the manager and the pitching coach, and, on some teams, the coach is responsible for all the pitching changes during a game.

Jim Turner, pitching coach for the New York Yankees, describes what he does in these terms: "A coach can help a pitcher develop a new pitch. He can work with him on his control, possibly helping him to spot some kink in his delivery. But mostly it's a matter of trying to keep a pitcher aware, keeping him refreshed on little things, keeping him informed on hitters, and getting him to relax. And, quite important, keeping him from getting down in the dumps, not allowing him to lose confidence in himself."

Take Tom Seaver as an example. In his first two years with the New York Mets, Seaver didn't have much of a curve to go with his fastball. Al (Rube) Walker, the Met pitching coach, suggested he make a change in the way he gripped the ball. Seaver had been gripping with the index finger and middle fingers together along one seam and releasing the ball off his fingertips. "Move the ball farther back in your hand," Walker told him. This change increased the ball's spin; it's curve became tighter and sharper.

Angel pitching coach Norm Sherry (left) with young Steve Kealey.

Met pitching coach Al Walker (left) and bullpen coach Joe Pignatano. Both are former catchers.

Sometimes pitching batting practice is the pitching coach's duty.

Besides being capable of instruction in any one of pitching's fundamentals, coaches have to be knowledgeable on the subject of training and conditioning, for it is they who supervise this aspect of the player's career. Of course, not all pitchers get the same amount of instruction or supervision. In the case of a skilled and experienced pitcher, a consistent winner, the coach's role may be limited. The pitcher knows what to do; he does it. The coach may simply watch the man, watch his arm motion and delivery for flaws in timing. If a problem does develop, the coach is expected to offer a solution.

Virtually all pitching coaches are baseball veterans, and they are usually former major league pitchers or catchers. It's not enough, however, that the coach knows the skills that go with pitching and knows how to teach them. He also has to understand the personalities of his pitchers. He has to know whom he must needle in order to get a good performance, and he has to know whom to leave alone.

Teacher, counselor, and cheerleader—that's the major league pitching coach.

TRAINING AND CONDITIONING

Running, running, and more running.

That's how pitchers get into condition. When they assemble at spring training late in February, they do more running than throwing the first few days. Throughout the season, they run before each game (unless they're going to pitch), and they run hard.

Running gets the legs in shape. While pitchers regard their arms as golden treasures, their legs rate almost as high in their esteem. A pitcher's legs are usually the first thing that tires in a game. When a pitcher becomes unsteady on his legs, his ability to control the ball diminishes, and the chances of his injuring his arm increase. That's why running is so important.

Pitchers must be on hand for spring training a week or so ahead of the rest of the squad. They begin their running drills right away. If they do any throwing at all, it's only for a few minutes at a time.

Spring training is also the time when pitchers are drilled in fundamentals. Most teams have several diamonds available, and squads are split into small groups, each supervised by a coach. In addition, there are extra batting cages, pitching mounds, and sliding pits for specialized instruction. Pitchers are schooled in throwing to the bases, the fundamentals

Running is the tried and proven method used to keep pitchers in condition.

of the delivery, covering first base, and all the other basics.

Bunting practice gets a good deal of attention. At the Mets training camp in St. Petersburg, Florida, a twenty-foot white line is chalked from home plate three feet inside and parallel to the third-base foul line. The area inside the lines is where a sacrifice bunt is supposed to end up. In a pitcher's bunting drill, each man has to be able to put five of ten balls within the two lines. When a man fails, he has "to take a hike"—run a lap around the infield.

Pitchers keep sharp as fielders through endless "pepper" games. Two or three or more line up side by side, and one throws to a batter ten to twenty feet away who bangs the ball back. In pepper games of days past, the batter would slam the ball hard in an effort to make the pitchers commit errors. Nowadays the batter hits hard but not too hard. Modern-day pitchers are considered too valuable for such antics.

Besides conditioning their legs and building their stamina, pitchers give special attention to the muscles of their upper body. Of particular importance is the triceps, the long muscle along the back of the upper arm. It's from the triceps that a pitcher gets the power to "push" the ball toward the plate. Some teams have their pitchers use pulley weights to

Pirate pitchers Lou Acosta (left) and Bob Veale drill in covering first base.

Jim (Mudcat) Grant (left) and slugger Willie Stargell perform calisthenics at the Pirates' training camp.

strengthen the triceps.

Once intrasquad games begin, each pitcher on the staff works about two innings in turn. Coaches watch their pitchers carefully and do not allow them to throw hard. But some men are so competitive they don't like anyone to hit their pitching, not even their teammates.

Understandably, pitchers are constantly worried about their arms. Many a pitcher, when he arises in the morning, extends his pitching arm and makes a windmill motion with it. He just wants to see how it feels.

Pain is not uncommon. After all, pitching a baseball is something the arm was never meant to do, especially in the case of pitching straight overhand. Try this test: Stand erect and let your arm hang naturally from your shoulder. Notice how the palm and elbow joint turn in. When you throw overhand, you strain the arm's muscles, ligaments, tendons, and joints in the opposite direction. This is what causes the pain. When a pitcher throws the ball 110-115 times, as he does in a well-pitched game, the pain can be intense. At its worst, it feels like someone has stabbed you in the upper shoulder. Rubdowns and rest help alleviate the pain.

Throughout the season, starting pitchers follow a fairly rigid training schedule. Suppose a pitcher starts a game on Sunday and goes the full nine innings. On Monday he will do light exercise to work the stiffness out of his legs. Often this involves field-

Houston's Larry Dierker works out on the "Exer-genie."

ing balls in the infield. On Tuesday he'll do wind sprints in the outfield. He's also likely to throw hard for ten minutes or so.

On Wednesday there's more hard running and maybe some light throwing. Thursday is like Monday. If he runs, it's only for a brief time. That day he also keeps the chart on the pitcher who works that day. On Friday he pitches again.

Of course, this regimen varies from team to team. Some managers prefer to have their starters pitch every four days instead of every five. There's less running in hot weather, and relief pitchers run less than starting pitchers because they have to be ready for virtually every game.

Keeping in condition from the opening of spring training to the end of the baseball season is no easy matter. The problem is the baseball schedule, for it quickly wearies the best conditioned athletes.

A typical segment of the schedule went like this for the Pittsburgh Pirates during 1971: The team completed a home stand on Thursday and met the following morning at the Pittsburgh airport for a flight to New York, which took one hour and twenty-three minutes. A chartered bus met the team at the airport and took them to the Hotel Commodore, a forty-minute ride. After the players checked in, they had lunch.

There was a night game scheduled against the Mets at Shea Stadium at 8:05. That meant the players had to be ready to board the team bus at 5:15

Sparky Lyle, a relief pitcher for the Red Sox, unlimbers before a game.

Fielding balls in the infield helps Tom Seaver loosen up.

P.M. in order to be at the ball park two hours before game time. (Players are not required to take the bus, but if they leave later and take a taxicab, they must pay their own way. Almost all take the bus.)

The game was over at 11:00 P.M. After they had showered and dressed, they boarded the bus once more. They were back at the hotel not long after midnight. They relaxed; they ate. Most were asleep by 2 A.M.

A game was scheduled the next day, a Saturday, at 2 P.M. The players had to be up at 9 A.M. in order to shower, dress, have breakfast, and be aboard the bus for a 10:15 departure.

There are rainouts, twi-night double-headers, Sunday doubleheaders, and extra-inning ball games that disrupt the scheduling. Time zone changes create problems. Then there are the airplane flights.

Teams charter planes, which means they lease or hire an entire aircraft and its crew. There is no scheduled departure time. The plane is always waiting.

The convenience factor, however, is offset by the rigors of air travel itself. Every player beyond the rookie stage can recite a catalog of what airline people call "incidents"—near collisions, engine failures, terrifying storms, periods of air turbulence, landings that curdle the blood, and delays, delays waiting to board, to take off, to land, and debark. Some players are as content in an aircraft as they are in their living rooms, but most approach air travel with apprehension.

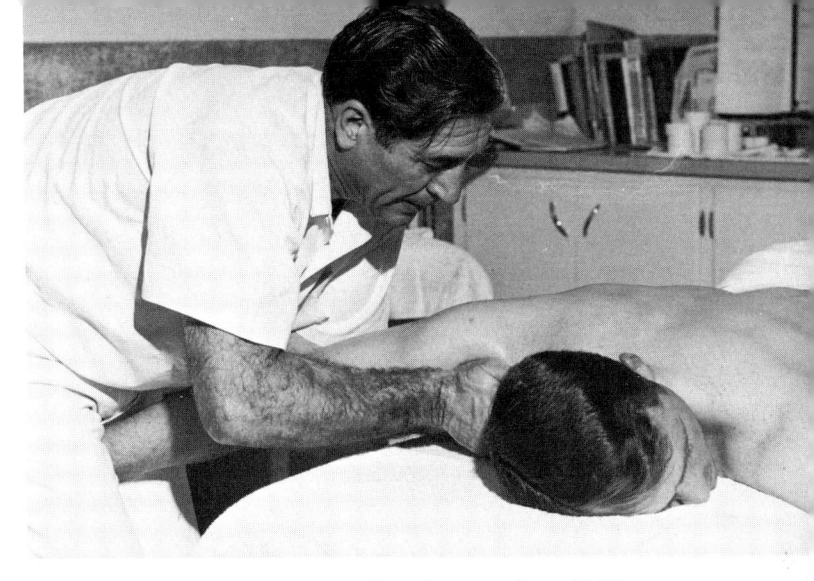

Montreal trainer Joe Liscio soothes the muscles of Mike Wegener's pitching arm.

All of these things take their toll. The season is not very long before insomnia and indigestion are as common as long sideburns. Sometimes "keeping in condition" is simply a matter of trying to get a good night's sleep.

It must be said, however, that the rigors of the schedule do not weigh quite so heavily on pitchers as they do on other players. A starting pitcher works one day and then rests three or four. For batters, a day off is rare.

PITCHING STATISTICS

There is one area in which major league baseball is acknowledged to be superior to professional football, basketball, and ice hockey, and that is in the statistical data it issues. From the standpoint of both the quantity of statistics and their richness of detail, no other sport comes close.

The statistical information for each game is compiled by the official scorer, who is selected from the corps of local newsmen covering the home team. He observes the game from the press box. When the game is over, he fills out a detailed report on a large form, the size of a page from a tabloid newspaper. The report gives the date of the game, where it was played, the names of the competing teams, the names of the umpires, the full score of the game and all the records of the individual players compiled according to the official scoring rules. (The rules, which include instructional information on how to keep score, are available from *The Sporting News*, 1212 N. Lindbergh Boulevard, St. Louis, Missouri, 63166, for sixty cents.)

Within thirty-six hours after the game, the scorer must send the report to the official statistician of the league involved. The Elias Sports Bureau in New York is the official statistician for the National League, and the Howe News Bureau in Chicago for the American League. These firms compile and certify all averages, percentages, and totals, and then issue the results to newspapers, magazines, and other clients, including the companies that print and distribute gum cards.

Of all of the hundreds upon hundreds of different types of baseball statistics, one above all others has

92

Left: **Year in, year out, Tom Seaver in the National League...**

...and Jim Palmer in the American are among the ERA leaders.

special meaning for pitchers. It is the earned run average—ERA.

The full name for this all important yardstick is "earned run average per nine-inning game." The official playing rules define an "earned run" as one "for which the pitcher is held accountable." This means that when a batter reaches base and advances and then scores by means of a safe hit, a sacrifice bunt or fly, stolen bases, putouts, fielder's choice, walks, hit batsmen, balks, or wild pitches, the run is to be designated as earned. It is not earned when the runner reaches base through an error or his advance is aided by an error.

To determine a pitcher's earned run average, divide the number of innings pitched into the number of earned runs allowed. (In case of portions or thirds of innings, take the nearest complete inning. Thus, 71⅓ innings becomes 71 innings, and 71⅔ innings becomes 72 innings). Then multiply the result by 9. For example, suppose a pitcher gave up 65 runs in 188 innings. His ERA would be figured in this manner:

$$\begin{array}{r} .345 \\ 188\overline{)65.000} \\ 564 \\ \overline{860} \\ 752 \\ \overline{1080} \\ 940 \\ \overline{140} \end{array} \qquad \begin{array}{r} .345 \\ \times 9 \\ \hline 3.105 \end{array}$$

In listing the ERA, only two decimal places are used. So in the case above, 3.11 would be the final statistic.

A pitcher's won-lost percentage can be important, too. To determine this statistic, divide the total number of games—that is, wins plus losses (but not ties)—into the number of victories, for that particular pitcher. Carry out the answer to three decimal places. Suppose a pitcher has a 20-12 record for the season. This would give him a total of 32 decisions, and his won-lost percentage would be figured like this:

```
            .625
       ─────────
    32 ) 20.000
         192
         ───
          80
          64
          ──
         160
         160
         ───
```

won-lost percentage: .625

The same holds true if you are figuring a pitcher's lifetime won-lost percentage. A pitcher with a 170-163 lifetime record would have a won-lost percentage of .511 (333 divided into 170).

While fans and newspapers are quick to hail a pitcher for winning a high number of games, or compiling a splendid won-lost percentage, baseball wise men declare that a pitcher's ERA gives a much more valid indication of the man's true ability. When a pitcher wins a considerable number of games, twenty or more, say, many factors are involved. Effective pitching is only one of them. Solid hitting and good fielding are two others, and a pitcher has no control over either of these.

A pitcher can lose an appalling number of games and still be a very good pitcher. His teammates' failure to hit or make putouts may be the overriding cause in many of his losses.

What constitutes a superior earned run average? Generally, one of 3.00 or less is considered excellent. But it depends. It depends on how well the other pitchers in the league perform. In 1968, the so-called "Year of the Pitcher," an ERA of 3.00 was not nearly so glittering as in 1969 or ensuing years.

The league that the pitcher represents and the quality of the hitting in that league must also be weighed. In the late 1960's and early 1970's, the National League had the better hitters. As a result, in one recent year only five National League pitchers could boast ERA's of less than 3.00, while eighteen pitchers in the American League could.

Sometimes a pitcher's total strikeouts or his strikeout percentage per inning are taken as evidence of his ability. An average of one strikeout per inning is said to indicate pitching excellence. However, more than a few experts say that an extraordinary number of strikeouts may only mean that the pitcher has one overpowering pitch—his strikeout pitch. He might have shortcomings in other areas.

The pitcher's ERA—that's the statistic that counts for him. It bears little relationship to the number of runs his team gets for him or fails to get. It has almost nothing to do with the fielding support he receives or doesn't receive. It's a statistic for which the pitcher alone is accountable. It's his "report card."

Vida Blue, with a splendid 1.82 ERA in 1971, won the American League's Cy Young Award and was also named the league's Most Valuable Player.

GREAT DAYS IN PITCHING

The skies were overcast and rain threatening on the afternoon of May 1, 1920, when Joe Oeschger, a big right-handed pitcher for the Boston Braves, took the mound at Braves Field to face the Brooklyn Dodgers. Leon Cadore, his pitching opponent, watched from the dugout steps as Oeschger fired the game's first pitch.

Baseball's longest day had begun. Through the dark afternoon the teams were to battle twenty-six innings without reaching a decision. What is so remarkable about the epic struggle is that both Oeschger and Cadore went the entire distance *Twenty-six innings; almost three complete games.* It is a standard of endurance that has never been equaled.

Oeschger was happy that he had been given the starting assignment. In a game against the Dodgers earlier in the season, he had been beaten, 1-0, in eleven innings, and Cadore had been the pitcher who had administered the defeat. Now Oeschger was getting a chance for revenge.

The Dodgers were the first to score. In the fifth inning, Oeschger, pitching too carefully to catcher Ernie Krueger, gave him a base on balls. Cadore then banged a sharp bounder back to Oeschger. In his eagerness to get a double play, Oeschger juggled the ball, but recovered in time to throw out Cadore at first base. Ivy Olsen's single scored Krueger.

Boston evened the score in the very next inning. With one out, Wally Cruise blasted a line-drive triple off the scoreboard in left field and came home on Tony Boeckel's single.

That was the end of the scoring. For the next twenty innings, Cadore with his curve and Oeschger with his fastball retired batter after batter, and no one crossed home plate.

There were a couple of threats. The Braves came close to scoring in the ninth inning when they filled the bases with one out, but Cadore got Charley Pick to hit into a double play.

The zeroes kept going up on the scoreboard. It was the Dodgers who threatened in the seventeenth. With one out and the bases filled, Rody Elliot grounded to Oeschger who threw to the plate for a forceout. Catcher Hank Gowdy's throw to first in an effort to get the double play was wide, and when first baseman Walter Holke juggled the ball, the runner from second rounded third and dashed for the plate. Suddenly Holke realized what was happening, and he fired the ball to Gowdy. The Boston catcher had to throw himself across the base line but he made the tag that stifled the rally.

By the eighteenth inning, Oeschger was beginning to feel the strain. His teammates urged him on. "Just one more inning," they kept telling him. "We'll get a run for you; don't worry."

As the afternoon wore on, darkness became more and more a problem. Ball parks were not lighted in those days. The hitters began to complain that they could not see the ball.

At the end of the twenty-sixth inning, umpire Barry McCormick, after conferring with the rival managers, called the game to a halt. Only one man protested, Ivy Olsen, the Dodgers' second baseman. "Give us one more inning," he pleaded.

"What for?" asked McCormick, who was as exhausted as the players.

"So we could say we played three full games in one afternoon."

"Not without miners' lamps on your caps," said McCormick.

```
           BROOKLYN              |            BOSTON
            AB  R  H  PO  A      |             AB  R  H  PO  A
Olson, 2b   10  0  1   5  8      | Powell, cf   7  0  1   8  0
Neis, rf    10  0  1   9  0      | Pick, 2b    11  0  0   6 11
Johnston, 3b 10 0  0   2  3      | Mann, lf    10  0  2   6  0
Wheat, lf    9  0  2   2  0      | Cruise, rf   9  1  1   4  0
Myers, cf    2  0  1   2  0      | Holke, 1b   10  0  2  42  1
Hood, cf     6  0  1   9  1      | Boeckel, 3b 11  0  3   1  7
Konetchy, 1b 9  0  1  30  0      | Mar'ville, ss 10 0  3   1  9
Ward, ss    10  0  0   5  3      | O'Neil, c    2  0  0   4  1
Krueger, c   2  1  0   4  3      | aChristenbury 1 0  1   0  0
Elliott, c   7  0  0   7  3      | Gowdy, c     6  0  1   6  1
Cadore, p   10  0  0   1 12      | Oeschger, p  9  0  1   0 11
 Totals     85  1  9  78 31      |  Totals     86  1 15  78 41
Brooklyn  000 010 000 000 000 000 000 000 00—1
Boston    000 001 000 000 000 000 000 000 00—1
```

aSingled for O'Neil in ninth. Runs batted in—Olson, Boeckel. Two-base hits—Maranville, Oeschger. Three base hit—Cruise. Stolen bases—Myers, Hood. Sacrifices—Hood, Oeschger, Powell, O'Neil, Holke, Cruise. Double plays—Olson and Konetchy; Oeschger, Holke and Gowdy. Bases on balls—Off Cadore 5, off Oeschger 4. Struck out—By Cadore 7, by Oeschger 7. Wild pitch —Oeschger. Left on bases—Brooklyn 11, Boston 16. Umpires— McCormick and Hart. Time of game—3 hours, 50 minutes. Official scorer—Shannon.

May 1, 1920: Joe Oeschger—Leon Cadore

Boston newspapers predicted that neither Oeschger or Cadore would ever pitch again. Both men took the game in stride, however.

Oeschger pitched again eight days later. "I did miss a turn," he told *The Sporting News* in 1970. "I would have been ready to work in rotation, but the next day I pulled a leg muscle running around the park and manager George Stallings let me skip a turn. But my arm was okay."

The record book shows that Oeschger won fifteen games that season, and the next season was the best of his career; his record was 20-14. Cadore also gathered 15 wins during the 1920 season, the highest winning total of his career.

Teams have come close to equaling the 26-inning record a number of times. The longest game in recent years took place in 1968, a 24-inning marathon between the New York Mets and the Houston Astros, a game the Astros won, 1-0. The rival managers used a combined total of thirteen pitchers. No one even considered trying to equal the endurance feat of Oeschger or Cadore. No pitcher ever does. Their dual achievement is likely to stand for as long as baseball is played.

No-hit, no-run games, while they don't occur with any great frequency, are not exactly rare. *The Little Red Book of Baseball* lists more than 175 of them. Many of these have been pitched by men of quite ordinary skills. John Kralick of the Twins, Len Johnson of the Astros, Dave Morehead of the Red Sox, and Clyde Wright of the Angels are among those who have hurled no-hitters in recent years. None of these men is considered Hall of Fame material.

Pitching two or more no-hitters is an unusual feat, but it has been done by sixteen different pitchers. Sandy Koufax pitched four no-hitters.

There have been a handful of pitchers who have tossed two no-hit games in one season. Jim Maloney of the Reds was the last to turn the trick. He did it in 1965.

But in all of baseball history there has only been one pitcher who served up two no-hit games in a row. His name was Johnny Vander Meer, a pitcher for the Cincinnati Reds. He performed his miracle feat in June, 1938.

Vander Meer, a lanky twenty-three-year-old, had joined the Reds at the tail end of the 1937 season after six rather undistinguished seasons in the minor leagues. The son of a Midland, New Jersey, stonemason who had come to the United States from Holland, Vander Meer was a fastballing left-hander who had control problems.

He compiled a 3-5 record with the Reds, and impressed manager Bill McKechnie enough to be invited to spring training the next year, 1938. McKechnie worked with Vandy in an effort to improve the young man's control, and even got him to change his pitching motion from sidearm to completely overhand. It didn't work; Johnny became wilder.

On the trip north, the Reds traveled on the same train with the Red Sox. The great Lefty Grove was in the final years of his career with the Boston team, and Vander Meer's erratic arm reminded Grove of his own pitching difficulties as a young major leaguer many years before.

Grove told Vandy he was able to solve his own control problem when he realized that he was releasing the ball too soon. "Make up your mind to follow through on every pitch," Grove said. Vander Meer accepted this advice. Soon after, he became a starting pitcher, then a winning pitcher, and ultimately a baseball immortal.

On Saturday, June 11, in a game played in Cincinnati, Johnny won headlines from coast to coast by beating the Boston Bees, 3-0, without allowing a base hit. Three men reached base, all on walks. It was Johnny's sixth win of the young season and boosted him into the league lead in strikeouts.

Four days later the Reds faced the Brooklyn Dodgers at Ebbets Field. Johnny was named to pitch. A sellout crowd of 38,748 jammed every corner of the ball park, but not just to see the young rookie who had surprised the baseball world with his no-hitter. There was another attraction. This was to be the first game to be played at night at Ebbets Field. Compared to the exciting newness of night baseball, Vandy was just a mere side attraction.

The Reds jumped into the lead with four runs in the fourth inning. Johnny, meanwhile, was mowing down Dodger batters. Little by little the interest of

BOSTON	AB	H	O	A	CINCINNATI	AB	H	O	A
G. Moore, rf	1	0	2	0	Frey, 2b	4	0	1	2
Fletcher, 1b	1	0	5	0	Berger, lf	3	1	2	0
Mueller	1	0	0	0	Goodman, rf	3	0	0	0
Coony, 1b-rf	3	0	4	0	M'Cormick, 1b	4	1	14	1
DiMaggio, cf	3	0	1	0	Lombardi, c	4	2	5	2
Cuccinello, 2b	2	0	1	3	Craft, cf	3	0	3	0
R. Reis, lf	3	0	3	0	Riggs, 3b	3	1	0	5
English, 3b	2	0	0	2	Myers, s	3	0	1	2
Riddle, c	3	0	5	0	V'D'Meer, p	3	1	1	2
Warstler, s	2	0	3	3	Totals	30	6	27	14
Kahle	1	0	0	0					
M'Fayden, p	2	0	0	0					
Maggert	1	0	0	0					
Totals	25	0	24	8					

Mueller batted for Fletcher in ninth.
Kahle batted for Warstler in ninth.
Maggert batted for MacFayden in ninth.

```
Boston         0 0 0  0 0 0  0 0 0—0
Cincinnati     0 0 0  1 0 2  0 0 *—3
```

Runs—Berger 2. Lombardi. Error—Cuccinello. Runs batted in —Goodman, Lombardi 2. Three-base hits—Berger, Riggs. Home run—Lombardi. Double plays—Cuccinello to Warstler to Cooney; Lombardi to McCormick. Bases on balls—Off MacFayden 1, Vander Meer 3. Struck out—By MacFayden 4, Vander Meer. Hit by pitcher—By MacFayden (Goodman). Umpires—Magerkurth, Parer and Moran. Time of game—1 h. 43 m.

June 11, 1938; Johnny Vander Meer

the crowd began to switch from the novelty of the lights to what the Cincinnati southpaw was doing. He was their hero by the sixth inning and they were urging him on with every pitch.

By the ninth inning, the crowd was watching each pitch with breathless anticipation. Buddy Hassett was the first batter to come to the plate in that inning. Swinging at the first pitch, Hassett banged the ball to Johnny's left. No problem. Johnny scooped the ball up in his glove and tagged Hassett as he raced toward first. A loud cheer went up from the crowd.

Johnny could feel the butterflies fluttering as Babe Phelps stepped in. Pitching too carefully, he walked Phelps on five pitches. Then he walked Cookie Lavagetto. Now Dolph Camilli, a dangerous man, was at the plate. Johnny poured over a strike.

Before Johnny could pitch again, Dodger manager Burleigh Grimes called time to send young Goody Rosen in to run for the chunky Phelps. It was the right move, but Grimes was booed for his efforts. Dodger fans were not interested in seeing their team win this night; they wanted Johnny to write baseball history.

When play resumed, Johnny's control deserted him. He walked Camilli on four straight pitches to fill the bases. The crowd was almost silent.

Now Bill McKechnie called time. He walked slowly to the mound to calm his young pitcher. "Heck, kid," McKechnie said, "they're more scared of that ball than you are. Just pour it in there."

Johnny buzzed across a strike to Ernie Koy, and then got the Dodger outfielder to hit a ground ball to Lew Riggs at third. Riggs made a perfect play, throwing to catcher Ernie Lombardi who made the force on Rosen.

The next man was the Dodger shortstop, a sticky little hitter named Leo Durocher. Johnny's first pitch to Durocher was a ball. Lombardi lumbered to the mound, placed that ball in Johnny's glove, and said, "Now, you're either going to give up a hit or you're not. So buzz that fast one right through there."

Vandy did as he was told. The next two pitches were blazing strikes. One strike to go! Vandy pumped and threw. Durocher swung early, slicing the ball toward the right field corner. As it curved foul, the crowd let out a collective sigh of relief.

Johnny took his time before pitching to Durocher again. Finally he stretched, kicked, and threw. Durocher swung and lifted a lazy fly into center field. The huge crowd roared happily even before Harry Craft made the catch.

Thousands of fans poured from the stands before the teams could run from the field. Johnny's teammates had to run interference to get him to the dressing room.

The season marked the beginning of a fine career for Johnny Vander Meer. It spanned fourteen seasons, and he won a total of 119 games. But it is the first year that stands out in his memory. No rookie has ever scaled such lofty heights, and very few pitchers have even come close.

Since 1900, seven pitchers have accomplished the monumental feat of facing only 27 batters in a no-run, no-hit performance. The perfect-game pitchers are:

Cy Young (Boston vs. Philadelphia, May 5, 1904)

Adrian Joss (Cleveland vs. Philadelphia, October 2, 1908)

Ernie Shore (Boston vs. Washington, June 23, 1917)

Charles Robertson (Chicago vs. Detroit, April 30, 1922)

Jim Bunning (Philadelphia vs. New York, June 21, 1964)

Sandy Koufax (Los Angeles vs. Chicago, September 9, 1965)

CINCINNATI	AB	H	O	A	BROOKLYN	AB	H	O	A
Frey, 2b	3	1	2	3	Cuyler, rf	2	0	1	0
Berger, lf	5	3	1	0	Coscarart, 2b	2	0	1	2
Goodman, rf	3	1	3	0	aBrack	1	0	0	0
McCormick, 1b	5	1	9	1	Hudson, 3b	1	0	1	0
Lombardi, c	3	0	9	0	Hassett, lf	4	0	3	0
Craft, cf	5	3	1	0	Phelps, c	3	0	9	0
Riggs, 3b	4	1	0	1	bRosen	0	0	0	0
Myers, s	4	0	0	2	Lavagetto, 3b	2	0	0	2
Vander Meer, p	4	1	2	4	Camilli, 1b	1	0	7	0
Totals	36	11	27	11	Koy, cf	4	0	4	0
					Durocher, ss	4	0	1	2
					Butcher, p	0	0	0	1
					Pressnell, p	2	0	0	0
					Hamlin, p	0	0	0	1
					cEnglish	1	0	0	0
					Tamulis, p	0	0	0	0
					Totals	27	0	27	8

aBatted for Coscarart in sixth; bRan for Phelps in ninth. cBatted for Hamlin in eighth.

Cincinnati   004 000 110—6
Brooklyn   000 000 000—0

Runs batted in—McCormick 3, Riggs, Craft, Berger. Two-base hit—Berger. Three-base hit—Berger. Home run McCormick. Stolen bases—Goodman. Left on bases—Cincinnati 11, Brooklyn 8. Bases on balls—Off Butcher 1, Vander Meer 8, Hamlin 3. Struck out by Butcher 1, Pressnell 3, Vander Meer 7, Hamlin 3. Hits off Butcher 5 in 2-2/3, Hamlin 2 in 1-2/3, Pressnell 4 in 3-2/3, Tamulis 0 in 1. Lossing pitcher, Butcher. Time 2:22.

June 15, 1938; Johnny Vander Meer

Jim Hunter (Oakland vs. Minnesota, May 8, 1968)

The Little Red Book of Baseball lists one other perfect game. It is more noteworthy than any of the others because it was a World Series game. It was pitched by tall, blue-eyed, brown-haired Don Larsen, an unheralded member of the New York Yankees' pitching staff. It came on October 6, 1956.

Larsen's career prior to the 1956 World Series was not outstanding by any means. After four years in the minors, he joined the hapless St. Louis Browns in 1953. His record was 7-12 that year, and 3-21 in 1954, the year the St. Louis franchise was switched to Baltimore. Two of Larsen's wins that season were against the New York Yankees, and that winter when New York and Baltimore engineered a seventeen-man trade, the largest in baseball history, the Yanks insisted on getting Larsen.

There must have been days when New York regretted the demand. Larsen proved so inept in the opening weeks of the 1955 season that the Yankees sent him to their Denver farm team. He returned on July 31 to win eight of nine games and help the Yankees win the pennant. Handed a starting assignment in the World Series against the Brooklyn Dodgers, Larsen was hit hard, lasting less than five innings, and ending up the losing pitcher.

In 1956 Larsen failed to finish five of his first seven starts, and his record was an unspectacular 7-5 by September. But in the final weeks of the season, he won four consecutive games to finish with an 11-5 record.

Again the Yankees faced the Dodgers in the Series. Brooklyn won the opening game, defeating Yankee ace Whitey Ford. Larsen started the second game and the Yankees got one run in the first inning and five runs in the second. He was smiling and confident as he strode to the mound in the bottom half of the inning. Maybe he was overconfident; maybe he eased up. Whatever the reason, he walked four batters, a transgression that helped trigger a five-run Dodger uprising, and caused Casey Stengel to replace him with Johnny Kucks.

"I figured I had blown my chance," Larsen was to say later. "I was sure I'd never get a chance to start in that Series again."

The Yankees won the fourth game to tie matters at two games apiece. Winning the fifth game was critical, but more so for the Yankees than the Dodgers. The Series was to shift to Brooklyn's tiny Ebbets Field for the sixth game, and there the hard-hitting Dodgers were almost invincible.

When Stengel announced that Larsen was to pitch, it came as a surprise. Stengel explained his decision to the press: "Larsen wasn't throwin' when he pitched in Brooklyn," Casey said. "He was just pushin' the ball up there. Maybe he was worried about the fences. I dunno. But he can pitch better. You'll see."

The game was scheduled to begin at 1 P.M. Since Stengel wanted his players in the clubhouse at least three hours before game time, it meant that Don had to get up at 8 A.M. He liked to sleep late, and when the alarm went off, it put him in a dark mood. He had only a cup of tea for breakfast, and then took a taxi to Yankee Stadium.

In the Yankee clubhouse, Larsen declined food, but drank some fruit juice. His sour disposition began to change once he started loosening up. His breaking pitches were much sharper than usual and everything he threw was right on target.

As he walked to the mound for the first inning, Larsen felt suddenly tense. He scanned the great tiered stands, packed to capacity. He threw his first pitch and the nervousness disappeared.

After three innings, Larsen knew that he was in for a battle. Neither he or Dodger pitcher Sal Maglie had allowed a hit.

Mickey Mantle jumped the Yanks into the lead in the fourth inning when he slammed one of Maglie's curveballs into the right-field seats, the first hit of the game. Larsen got by the bottom of the inning without incident, but in the fifth inning there were some fireworks. Gil Hodges lashed one of Larsen's pitches into left center. It looked like it might be going for extra bases, but Mickey Mantle managed to grab it with a splendid backhand catch. Later in the inning, Sandy Amoros nailed one of Larsen's pitches into the stands in right field. It was foul by only a foot.

In the bottom of the sixth, Larsen, working with a two-run lead, set the Dodgers down in order once more. As he walked toward the dugout, he could hear the fans buzzing. The pressure was beginning to build.

Larsen retired the Dodgers one-two-three in the seventh and the eighth. The crowd was now hanging breathlessly on every pitch.

When Larsen walked to the mound to begin the ninth inning, he was aware that every eye was on him. He got Carl Furillo to fly to right field and Roy Campanella to ground to second. The crowd gasped as big Dale Mitchell was announced as a pinch hitter for Maglie. As Mitchell, one of the best pinch hitters in baseball, advanced toward home plate swinging a pair of bats, Larsen turned toward center field and raised his face to the sky. "Please help me," he seemed to be saying.

Larsen's first pitch was a ball. His heart sank. "Oh, no," he thought. "I've been ahead of hitters all day. What a time to lose my control."

The next pitch was a strike. In the Yankee bullpen, Larsen's roommate, pitcher Rip Coleman, turned his back on the field, afraid to watch what was happening.

Another strike.

Larsen removed his cap and wiped his brow with his right sleeve. Catcher Yogi Berra signaled for a fastball. Larsen delivered. Mitchell took a vicious swing, getting just a piece of the ball. It caromed to the backstop.

Larsen breathed a deep sigh. "A half an inch higher and it would have been a line drive," he thought.

Again Berra signaled for a fastball. Larsen fired. Mitchell started to swing, then held up. Umpire Babe Pinelli's right hand shot into the air. "Strike three!" he roared.

Mitchell whirled around to argue the call but it was a poor time to launch a protest. Yankee Stadium was a bedlam. Yogi Berra had sprinted toward the mound and leaped on Larsen. Then the other players and a swarm of fans surrounded him, and carried him from the field.

In the clubhouse Larsen was almost overcome with emotion. His fingers trembled when he tried to light a cigarette. "I don't believe what happened to me," he said. "I don't believe it. I'm shaking like a leaf. How can I answer questions? I can't think."

He shook his head in disbelief. "I can't believe it," he said. And he kept repeating it over and over.

One other perfect performance must be mentioned. In some ways it was even more masterful than the game Don Larsen pitched or any of the others. On the night of May 26, 1959, Harvey Haddix of the Pittsburgh Pirates pitched twelve perfect innings against the Milwaukee Braves, retiring 36 batters in a row, an unprecedented feat in baseball

DODGERS	AB	R	H	O	A	E	YANKEES	AB	R	H	O	A	E
Reese, ss	3	0	0	4	2	0	Bauer, rf	4	0	1	4	0	0
Gilliam, 2b	3	0	0	2	0	0	Collins, 1b	4	0	1	7	0	0
Snider, cf	3	0	0	1	0	0	Mantle, cf	3	1	1	4	0	0
Robinson, 3b	3	0	0	2	4	0	Berra, c	3	0	0	7	0	0
Hodges, 1b	3	0	0	5	1	0	Slaughter, lf	2	0	0	1	0	0
Amoros, lf	3	0	0	3	0	0	Martin, 2b	3	0	1	3	4	0
Furillo, rf	3	0	0	0	0	0	McDougald, ss	2	0	0	0	2	0
C'panella, c	3	0	0	7	2	0	Carey, 3b	3	1	1	1	1	0
Maglie, p	2	0	0	0	1	0	Larsen, p	2	0	0	0	1	0
aMitchell	1	0	0	0	0	0	Totals	26	2	5	27	8	0
Totals	27	0	0	24	10	0							

Dodgers (N.)   000 000 000—0
Yankees (A.)   000 101 00*—2

aCalled out on strikes for Maglie in ninth. Runs batted in—Mantle, Bauer. Home run—Mantle. Sacrifice hit—Larsen. Double plays—Reese and Hodges; Hodges, Campanella, Robinson, Campanella and Robinson. Left on base—Dodgers 0, Yankees 3. Bases on balls—Off Maglie 2 (Slaughter, McDougald). Struck out—By Larsen 7 (Gilliam, Reese, Hodges, Campanella, Snider, Maglie, Mitchell), by Maglie 5 (Martin, Collins 2, Larsen, Bauer). Runs and earned runs—Off Larsen 0-0, off Maglie 2-2. Winner—Larsen. Loser—Maglie. Umpires—Pinelli (N.L.) at plate; Soar (A.L.) first base; Boggess (N.L.) second base; Napp (A.L.) third base; Gorman (N.L.) left field; Runge (A.L.) right field. Time—2:06. Attendance—64,519.

October 8, 1956; Don Larsen

history. Yet to find Haddix's name in baseball's record books you must search the footnotes. The *tour de force* has all but been forgotten because Haddix had the great misfortune to wind up the losing pitcher.

Not a big man—5-foot-9, 160 pounds—Haddix had no blazing fastball, but he could throw hard and had a fine assortment of curves. Control was his chief weapon, however. He could put the ball precisely where he wanted to.

Haddix had arrived on the major league scene

with the St. Louis Cardinals in 1952 and the next year had won twenty games. That same season he had pitched a no-hitter for eight innings against the Philadelphia Phillies. The first hitter in the ninth slapped a single into right field.

That was the closest Haddix had come to a no-hit performance until the spring night in 1959 when, wearing the uniform of the Pittsburgh Pirates, he took the mound against the Braves in Milwaukee. His curveball was nipping the corners and he had masterful control. The nearest thing to a base hit during the first nine innings was a line drive by Johnny Logan in the third. Dick Schofield the Pittsburgh shortstop, speared it with a leaping catch.

Lew Burdette, the Milwaukee pitcher, was almost as tough. He had given up several hits, and the Pirates had come close to scoring a number of times, but Burdette had managed to hold them off.

In the tenth inning, the Braves were again unable to get a man to first, and the Pirates failed to get a run. The same thing happened in the eleventh and twelfth innings. The thirteenth inning started the same way, with Burdette setting the Pirates down wihout allowing them to score.

Haddix's face was grim with frustration as he went to the mound in the bottom half of the thirteenth. The first man to face him was Felix Mantilla. He slashed a grounder to third baseman Don Hoak, who threw into the dirt at the feet of first baseman Rick Nelson. Mantilla was safe. The error snapped the perfect string. But Haddix's no-hit game was still alive.

Ed Matthews sacrificed the fleet Mantilla to second. Hank Aaron, the league's leading hitter, was walked intentionally. Up stepped Joe Adcock. On the second pitch, Adcock connected, sending a towering drive toward right center field that barely cleared the fence. With one blow, Haddix had lost his no-hitter and the baseball game.

There was wild confusion following Adcock's homer. Hank Aaron, in his jubilation, cut across the diamond without touching second base. Adcock rounded second and passed Aaron. By this time, the field was mobbed with players, and they sent Aaron back to touch third and then home. Ultimately Aaron was ruled out. Adcock was given credit for a double and the Braves a 1-0 victory.

The score was unimportant. What really mattered was that Harvey Haddix had retired 36 men in a row—and lost.

Afterward in the Pirate dressing room, Haddix sat in front of his locker and dolefully answered reporters' questions. One of the newsmen told Haddix of the history-making nature of his performance, that never before had a pitcher worked more than ten perfect innings.

"Really!" exclaimed Haddix. "Well, what do you know about that!"

Then suddenly the sparkle left his eyes and his shoulders slumped. "But we lost," he murmured.

	PITTSBURGH					MILWAUKEE			
	AB	R	H	RBI		AB	R	H	RBI
Schofield, ss	6	0	3	0	O'Brien, 2b	3	0	0	0
Virdon, cf	6	0	1	0	bRice	1	0	0	0
Burgess, c	5	0	0	0	Mantilla, 2b	1	1	0	0
Nelson, 1b	5	0	2	0	Mathews, 3b	4	0	0	0
Skinner, lf	5	0	1	0	Aaron, rf	4	1	0	0
Mazeroski, 2b	5	0	1	0	Adcock, 1b	5	0	1	2
Hoak, 3b	5	0	2	0	Covington, lf	4	0	0	0
Mejias, rf	3	0	1	0	Crandall, c	4	0	0	0
aStuart,	1	0	0	0	Pafko, cf	4	0	0	0
Christopher, rf	1	0	0	0	Logan, ss	4	0	0	0
Haddix, p	5	0	1	0	Burdette, p	4	0	0	0
Totals	47	0	12	0	Totals	38	2	1	2

aFlied out for Mejias in 10th; bFlied out for O'Brien in 10th.

```
Pittsburgh    000 000 000 000 0—0
Milwaukee     000 000 000 000 2—2
```

Two out when winning run scored.
E—Hoak. A—Pittsburgh 13, Milwaukee 21. DP—Logan and Adcock; Mathews, O'Brien, Adcock; Adcock, Logan. LOB—Pittsburgh 8, Milwaukee 0. 2B Hit—Adcock, Sacrifice—Mathews.

	IP	H	R	ER	BB	SO
Haddix (L, 3-2)	12-2/3	1	2	1	0	8
Burdette (W, 8-2)	13	12	0	0	0	2

Umpires—Smith, Dascoli, Secory, Dixon.
Time—2:54. Attendance—19,194

May 26, 1959; Harvey Haddix

One of pitching's greatest days belongs to the very recent past. At New York's Shea Stadium on the afternoon of April 22, 1970, Tom Seaver of the Mets zoomed a knee-high fastball past Al Ferrara of the San Diego Padres to create a pitching masterpiece. When Ferrara, the last hitter of the game, swung and missed, he became Seaver's nineteenth strikeout victim and tenth in a row.

Nineteen strikeouts tied the major league record established by Steve Carlton of the Cardinals on September 15, 1969. Ten strikeouts in a row established a record.

The Mets were leading 2-1 in the sixth inning when Ferrara struck out to become Seaver's tenth victim. No one had a hint of what was to come. While the boyish-faced Seaver had allowed only two hits, one a home run to Ferrara, he was not overpowering the batters. What people didn't realize, however, was that Seaver himself was unaware of how many strikeouts he had posted. Manager Gil Hodges wasn't aware either.

When Seaver went out to the mound in the eighth inning, pitching coach Rube Walker turned to Hodges in the dugout. "I'll bet people don't realize how many strikeouts Tom has," said Walker.

"Eleven?" Hodges asked.

"No," said Walker. "He has thirteen."

"You're kidding!" Hodges said, and he began counting them up.

Bob Barton, lead-off batter in the eighth inning, took a called third strike. Ramon Webster, a pinch hitter for the San Diego pitcher, went down swinging. So did the next man, Mike Corkins.

Corkins was Seaver's fifteenth victim, which tied the Met club record. The news was flashed on the huge Shea Stadium message board.

"I thought I had ten or eleven," Seaver was to say later. "I didn't know I had fifteen until I saw it on the scoreboard. When I knew I did, I really tried for sixteen. I wanted the club record."

Tom's try was successful. Ivan Murrell, batting for Jose Arcia, swung and missed a third strike.

In the last of the eighth, the Mets went down quickly. Seaver, eager to get started, hurried to the mound. He was thinking about the record, yes, but his primary concern was Al Ferrara, who was to be the third man to bat in the inning. He had reached Seaver for a home run earlier in the game. Tom, with only a one-run lead, didn't want it to happen again.

Van Kelly was the first man to face Seaver. When he went down swinging on Tom's third pitch, it marked only the fifth time in major league history that a pitcher had struck out eight batters in succession. Clarence Gaston looked at a third strike, and Tom had nine in a row.

Now Ferrara was at the plate. Seaver was well aware the record was within his grasp—and he wanted it.

His first pitch was a slider on the outside corner. Ferrara stood motionless. "Strike!" umpire Harry Wendelstedt called out, and his right arm went up. A second slider missed the plate.

Seaver came back with a fastball. Ferrara swung and missed. Now Seaver was in the driver's seat, yet he wasn't bursting with confidence.

"I was still worried about him hitting it out," Tom said later. "I had to challenge him. I just let a fastball rip."

Rip it did. And Seaver had the record.

SAN DIEGO	AB	R	H	RBI	E	NEW YORK	AB	R	H	RBI	E
Arcia, ss	3	0	0	0	0	Agee, cf	3	1	1	0	0
Murrell, ph	1	0	0	0	0	Harrelson, ss	3	1	2	1	0
Roberts, p	0	0	0	0	0	Boswell, 2b	4	0	1	1	0
Kelly 3b	4	0	0	0	0	Jones, lf	4	0	0	0	0
Gaston, cf	4	0	0	0	0	Shamsky, rf	2	0	0	0	0
Ferrara, lf	3	1	1	1	0	Swoboda, rf	1	0	0	0	0
Colbert, 1b	3	0	0	0	0	Foy, 3b	2	0	0	0	0
Campbell, 2b	3	0	1	0	0	Kranepool, 1b	2	0	0	0	0
Morales, rf	3	0	0	0	0	Grote, c	3	0	0	0	0
Barton, c	2	0	0	0	0	Seaver, p	3	0	0	0	0
Corkins, p	2	0	0	0	0	Totals	27	2	4	2	0
Webster, ph	1	0	0	0	0						
Slocum, ss	0	0	0	0	0						
Totals	29	1	2	1	0						

San Diego 010 000 000—1
New York 101 000 00x—2

San Diego	IP	H	R	ER	BB	SO
Corkins (L. 0-2)	7	4	2	2	5	5
Roberts	1	0	0	0	0	2
New York	IP	H	R	ER	BB	SO
Seaver (W. 3-0)	9	2	1	1	2	19

LOB—San Diego 3, New York 6. 2B—Boswell. 3B—Harrelson. HR—Ferrara (1). SB—Agee. U—Venzon, Secory, Engel and Wendelstedt. T—2:14. A—14,197.

April 22, 1970; Tom Seaver

THE GREATEST PITCHERS

"It looked about the size of a watermelon seed and *hissed* at you as it passed." This was the way the immortal Ty Cobb described Walter Johnson's fastball.

Johnson used his fastball to earn a reputation as one of pitching's all-time greats. More than a few experts declare that he was the finest pitcher the game has known, and the statistics he achieved support such an argument. In a twenty-one-year career with the Washington Senators that ended in 1927, Johnson started and completed more games than any other pitcher. He won 414 games, more than any other pitcher except Cy Young. He struck out 3,508 batters, almost a thousand more than the next man on the list. He pitched 113 shutouts, another record.

Johnson never used his blazing speed to intimidate. If he ever brushed back a man, history has made no note of it. He just leaned back and fired. Even if the pitch was over the heart of the plate, it didn't matter much, because batters were helpless to do anything.

"You might know it was coming," said Casey Stengel, whose playing career almost paralleled Johnson's, "but you couldn't hit it."

What is remarkable about Johnson's accomplishments is that they were achieved with a team that often finished deep down in the standings. The Senators were last or next to last seven times in John-

Walter Johnson

son's tenure with the club. Countless times, errors by his teammates cost Johnson victories, yet he never complained. Once, Clyde Milan, a usually dependable outfielder, dropped a fly ball in the eleventh inning that caused Johnson to lose, 1-0. In the clubhouse afterward, reporters told Johnson that he had every right to be angry. "Oh, I don't think so," Johnson said. "You know Clyde doesn't do that very often."

Johnson, like many players of his day, was a farm boy. Humboldt, Kansas, was where he was born. He was nineteen when he joined the Senators in 1920. He once said he was "the greenest rookie there ever was." In those days baseball parks did not always have dressing rooms. After a game the players took a bus back to the hotel to shower and dress. Johnson was unaware of this practice. After his first appearance for the Senators, he left the park and strolled down Pennsylvania Avenue, followed by an amused crowd.

It wasn't until Johnson was thirty-six that he got a chance to pitch in a World Series. His fastball was no longer quite so lethal, but he had developed a fine curve to go with his marvelous control. He started and lost the first and fifth series games, but he won the seventh and deciding contest in a relief appearance.

Johnson's last year with the Senators as a player was 1927, but he returned in 1929 to manage the team for three seasons. He later managed the Cleveland Indians. Johnson was generally unsuccessful as a manager, but this phase of his career in no way dimmed the brilliance of his pitching achievements. *The Official Encyclopedia of Baseball* calls Johnson's record ". . . the finest ever assembled by a pitcher after the turn of the century."

Among men who know baseball best, it is generally agreed that Walter Johnson was one of the greatest pitchers the game has ever known. Who were the others? The question often causes hot debate. There is one way of settling the matter, however. As part of its centennial celebration in 1969, baseball sought to establish the names of the game's greatest players. Fans, sportswriters, and sportscasters were polled. These pitchers were named as baseball's best:

Greatest right-handed pitchers ever: Walter Johnson, Cy Young, and Christy Mathewson.

Greatest left-handed pitchers ever: Lefty Grove, Sandy Koufax, and Carl Hubbell.

The career of Christopher (Christy or Matty) Mathewson was built on a pitch called the "fadeaway," a curveball that broke down and toward a right-handed batter. Today it would be termed a screwball. Mathewson was the one who originated the pitch, and, fittingly, he used it with sheer brilliance.

In his seventeen seasons of major league baseball, Mathewson averaged slightly more than 21 wins per

Christy Mathewson

season. In three consecutive years, 1903-1905, he won 30 or more games, and in 1908 he won 37.

The 1905 World Series saw Matty's greatest pitching performance. He almost single-handedly led his team, the New York Giants, to victory over the Philadelphia Athletics, pitching three victories in the five games, all shutouts. Christy hurled in four World Series, and compiled a glittering 1.15 for an ERA.

There were some years when Christy was the only dependable pitcher on the Giants staff, and manager John McGraw used him in game after game. In 1908, Matty appeared in 56 games, pitching 391 innings. He had no choice but to become skilled in pacing himself. Instead of trying to blow the ball by the batter on every pitch, Matty would coast, allowing batters to hit the ball and even reach base. He once pitched a 14-hit shutout. But anytime the pressure mounted, Matty was superb. Significantly, his autobiography was titled, *Pitching in a Pinch*.

Matty's lifetime record of National League victories, 373, was equaled by only one other pitcher, Grover Cleveland Alexander. He lost but 188, giving him a won-lost percentage of .665.

While Matty pitched during a scruffy, ragtag period in baseball history, he himself projected an All-American-boy image, and was perhaps the first professional athlete to do so. He was the idol of countless youngsters and when the Giants were on the road, and their train stopped at a station, a cluster of boys would often form to hear a few words from Christy or receive a wave. He was the most photographed player of his time.

Matty was born on August 12, 1880, in Factoryville, Pennsylvania. He did his first pitching for the YMCA in Scranton. The Giants acquired him from Norfolk of the Virginia League, where he registered 22 victories against only two losses.

Once Matty became established with the Giants, he conducted an insurance business with headquarters in New York. It grew to be a very successful enterprise. Matty always dressed to fit his off-the-field role, and in one picture he is shown wearing a wing collar and a necktie with a huge knot.

Matty died when he was relatively young, at forty-five, and under tragic circumstances. When the United States entered World War I, Matty became a captain in the Chemical Warfare Division, and was assigned to a training station in France where recruits were instructed in the use of gas masks. Real gas was used in the training drills, and Matty was often the last to don his mask. His lungs were damaged as a result, which made him easy prey to tuberculosis, the disease which took his life in 1925.

Of the countless baseball records that have been established, two seem absolutely unreachable. One is Ty Cobb's record of 4,191 base hits. Few players ever reach the 3,000 mark. The other is a pitching record established by Denton True (Cy) Young. Between the years 1890 and 1911, Cy Young won an incredible 511 games. It would take a miracle to win that many games today.

Cy was a right-hander, and, at 6-foot-2, 210

Cy Young

pounds, a big man for his day. There were periods in his career during which he pitched every other day, yet he never seemed to suffer from a sore arm. Additional evidence of his indestructibility is the fact that he pitched in more games than other pitchers (906), and pitched for more years than any other (23).

Cy hailed from the hills of Tuscarawas County in eastern Ohio and was all farm boy. The cuffs of his trousers ended well above his ankles and his shirt sleeves hung over his wrists. He liked wearing his low-crowned derby, even if it was too small.

Cy's fastball was his strikeout pitch. Its power earned him his nickname. In the spring of 1890, the owner of the Canton team in the Tri-State League asked Young to try out. Eager to impress, Cy threw the ball as hard as he could. One of his steaming fastballs eluded the catcher and ripped through some seats in the grandstand. An onlooker said it looked like a cyclone had struck. So they called Young "Cyclone," and later it was shortened to "Cy."

Cy's fastball won him a job with the Canton team, but the league failed before the season ended. The owner of the team sold Young's contract to Cleveland for three hundred dollars and a new suit of clothes. Cy pitched eight full seasons for Cleveland, never winning fewer than 21 games and one season he won 36.

Following two years with St. Louis, Cy signed with Boston in the "new" American League. He remained with Boston for eight years, winning 33 games in his first season and 32 the next.

Cy pitched three no-hit games during his career, one of them a perfect game. He appeared in baseball's first World Series, in 1903, pitching two victories for the Boston Red Sox in their conquest of the Pittsburgh Pirates.

The late Lee Allen, official historian for the National Baseball Hall of Fame for many years, once asked Cy to explain how he was able to remain such a dominant figure in baseball for so long a period. This was Young's answer:

"To begin with, I had a good arm and legs. You have to have good legs to pitch, and I always took care of them. When I would go to spring training I would never touch a ball for the first three weeks. Just would do a lot of walking and running. I never did any unnecessary throwing. I figured the old arm had just so many throws in it and there wasn't any use wasting them.

"Like, for instance, I never warmed up ten, fifteen, minutes before a game like most pitchers do. I'd loosen up for maybe three, four minutes. Five at the outside. And I never went to the bullpen. Oh, I'd relieve all right, plenty of times, but I went right from the bench to the box and I'd take a few warm-up pitches and then I'd be ready.

"Then I had good control. I aimed to make the batter hit the ball, and I made as few pitches as possible. That's why I was able to work every other

Lefty Grove

day. That and having good legs and keeping them good."

Cy was forty-five and with the Boston Braves when he decided it was time to retire. His arm was still sound and capable of whipping the ball across the plate. However, he had developed a paunch, and bunted balls were what made him decide to quit. "The boys are taking unfair advantage of me," he said. "They know this stomach of mine makes it difficult for me to field bunts, so they're laying the ball down instead of swinging."

Cy returned to his home at Peoli, Ohio, and occupied himself with farm chores. He frequently appeared at Old Timers' Day celebrations until his death in 1955 at eighty-eight. Not long before he died, Cy received a letter inquiring about the fastball speed of two of his pitching contemporaries, Amos Rusie and Walter Johnson. "Do not believe," Cy wrote in reply, "that either one was quite up to me in speed."

Many baseball men call Robert (Lefty) Grove the ultimate in southpaws. He won 300 games and lost only 141 in a brilliant career which began with the Philadelphia Athletics in 1925 and ended with the Boston Red Sox in 1941. Grove led the American League in winning percentage five times, in earned run average nine times, and in strikeouts seven times.

Grove was born in Lonaconing, Maryland, on March 6, 1900. He learned to throw with a homemade baseball. He and his chums would take a cork, wind it tightly with yarn from an unraveled sock, and then cover it with black tape.

Grove developed so much speed that it caused a problem. There was no catcher in his neighborhood who could handle his pitches, so Grove had to play first base. When a boy was finally found who could hold what he threw, Grove vaulted to fame.

As a tall, gangly twenty-year-old, Grove joined the Baltimore Orioles, members of the International League at the time, where he was to spend five years. After the 1924 season, in which he won 27 games, Grove was sold to the Athletics for a record price—$100,600, the extra six hundred dollars being added to surmount the previous record.

Lefty had control problems in his first two seasons in the major leagues, but in 1927 he won 20 games, and he never failed to win at least 20 games a season for the next six years. The 1931 season was his best. He won 31 games, including 16 in a row, and lost only 4. His streak of 16, which tied a league record, came to an end when a substitute outfielder dropped an easy fly ball, allowing the only run of the day to score. In World Series competition, Lefty had a 4-2 record and a splendid 1.75 ERA.

Midway in his career Grove injured his arm and soon after was sold to the Red Sox. He lacked his blazing speed, but developed an excellent curveball and a variety of change-of-pace pitches. This assortment enabled him to reach his goal of 300 wins.

Grove hated to lose. On the field he was all business. Once a reporter asked him to describe some of the humorous things he had seen in baseball. Grove looked at the man stonily, then replied, "I never saw anything funny about the game."

Carl Hubbell, a tall, skinny leftie with beetling eyebrows, had a fitting nickname—"King." King Carl he was called. In his sixteen-year career with the New York Giants, Hubbell reigned supreme in the National League, experiencing only one losing season, that in 1940, when his record was 11-12.

Hubbell was famous for his screwball. He discovered how to throw the pitch by accident in spring

Carl Hubbell

training with the Oklahoma City team in 1925. Hubbell was trying to develop a sinker, but found that if he let the ball come off his middle finger, and turned his wrist, it would veer to the side instead of sinking.

Hubbell's career, in which he won a total of 253 games, was studded with brilliant days. He pitched a no-hit game against Pittsburgh in 1929. He pitched an 18-inning shutout against St. Louis in 1933, yielding only six hits, no walks, and pitching twelve perfect innings.

Hubbell's best remembered feat came in the 1934 All Star game. The American League boasted a murderous array of hitters that year, but Hubbell handled them like schoolboys. In the first inning, after Charlie Gehringer had singled and Heine Manush had walked, Hubbell struck out Babe Ruth, Lou Gehrig, and Jimmy Foxx. He took the mound in the second inning and continued the string, striking out Al Simmons and Joe Cronin. Ruth . . . Gehrig . . . Foxx . . . Simmons . . . Cronin—five of baseball's most lethal sluggers, and Hubbell had struck them out one after another.

Two years later, in 1936, Hubbell won 16 games in a row, and then won his first eight in 1937, giving him a total of 24 consecutive victories, a record that still stands.

Hubbell was born in Carthage, Missouri, on June 22, 1933, and grew up on an Oklahoma pecan farm. He was twenty-two when he began throwing the screwball. The pitch puts excessive strain on the elbow and Hubbell did not escape the consequences. He experienced pain and swelling in the latter stages of his career, and ultimately had to undergo surgery for the removal of bone chips in his left elbow.

In Christy Mathewson's time, the screwball was called the fadeaway. In Hubbell's day it was known as the butterfly. Now it is often called the screwjie. No matter what the name, Hubbell threw the pitch with more devastating effect than anyone before or since.

Sandy Koufax of the Los Angeles Dodgers was an outstanding pitcher of more recent times. His career was cut short by an arthritic elbow in 1966, a year he won 27 games and turned in a 1.73 ERA. Over his career, Koufax won 165 games, not a noteworthy total, but the record book attests to Koufax's greatness.

A left-hander, Koufax led the National League in earned run average for five consecutive years (1962-1966), a feat not equaled before or since. While his victory total was not high, his won-lost percentage of .655 (165 games won; 87 lost) was one of the best in baseball history, better than Walter Johnson's or Cy Young's. Only three pitchers who won 150 games or more have better won-lost percentages than Koufax. They are Christy Mathewson, Lefty Grove, and Whitey Ford.

Koufax's greatest feats were as a strikeout artist. He averaged more than one strikeout per inning over his career (2,396 strikeouts; 2,325 innings). No other pitcher has ever done this. The record for strikeouts in a single season (383) is Koufax's. Only Koufax was able to strike out 300 or more men in three different seasons. Only Koufax was able to strike out 18 batters in nine-inning games on two different occasions. He also struck out ten or more batters in 97 different games, another record.

Consider what he did in the category of no-hit games. Walter Johnson had one no-hit game and Christy Mathewson had two. Koufax had four of them, and the last, against the Chicago Cubs in 1965, was a perfect game.

What is remarkable about all of this is that Koufax was not the type of pitcher who overwhelmed the batter. Of course, he had great speed and "stuff," but his strikeouts were more the result of his overall effectiveness, his knowledge, his shrewdness, and his great pitching "sense."

In the final stages of his career, an enormous amount of courage was also involved. Because of an arthritic left elbow, every throw caused him agonizing pain. There were times he could not raise his arm high enough to hail a taxicab without wincing.

In his last season, Koufax had to receive cortisone injections into the elbow joint and fluid had to be drained from it constantly. He had to pack the arm in ice and take pain-killing drugs before games to reduce the swelling. The condition was incurable.

Doctors told him that if he continued pitching there was a chance the arm might become permanently crippled.

There have been other great pitchers—Charlie (Old Hoss) Radbourn, who turned in a 60-12 record in 1884; Grover Cleveland Alexander, whose total of 373 games won equaled the mark established by Christy Mathewson; Dizzy Dean, the last pitcher before Denny McLain to win 30 games in a season; and Bob Feller, whose incredible fastball earned him a reputation as baseball's pre-eminent pitcher of the 1940's. But the men profiled here—Johnson . . . Mathewson . . . Young . . . Grove . . . Hubbell . . . Koufax—were something special.

Sandy Koufax

ALL-TIME PITCHING RECORDS

Most games, lifetime
1,045—Hoyt Wilhelm (through 1971)
 906—Cy Young
 804—Roy Face

Most games, season
 90—Wayne Granger, Cincinnati, 1969 (all relief)
 88—Wilbur Wood, Chicago, AL, 1968 (all relief)
 84—Ted Abernathy, Chicago, NL, 1965 (all relief)

Most complete games, lifetime
 751—Cy Young
 639—Pud Galvin
 557—Tim Keefe

Most complete games, season
 75—Will White, Cincinnati, 1879
 73—Charles Radbourn, Providence, NL, 1884
 72—Guy Hecker, Louisville, AA, 1884

Lowest earned run average, lifetime
 1.82—Ed Walsh
 1.88—Adrian Joss
 2.06—Mordecai (Three Finger) Brown

Lowest earned run average, season (200 or more innings)
 1.01—Emil (Dutch) Leonard, Boston, 1914
 1.04—Mordecai (Three Finger) Brown, Chicago, NL, 1906
 1.09—Walter Johnson, Washington, 1913

Most years leading league, earned run average
 9—Bob (Lefty) Grove

Most games won, lifetime
 511—Cy Young
 413—Walter Johnson
 373—Grover Alexander
 373—Christy Mathewson

Most games won, season
 60—Charles (Old Hoss) Radbourn, Providence, NL, 1884
 42—Charles Baldwin, Detroit, 1886
 41—Jack Chesbro, New York, AL, 1904

Most years leading league, games won
 8—Warren Spahn

Most consecutive games won
 24—Carl Hubbell, New York, NL, 1936-1937

Most years, 20 or more wins
 16—Cy Young

**Highest percentage, lifetime
(100 or more decisions)**
 .717 (109-43) —Spud Chandler
 .690 (236-106)—Whitey Ford
 .690 (147-68) —Dave Foutz

**Highest percentage, season
(15 or more decisions)**
 .947 (18-1)—Roy Face, Pittsburgh, 1959
 .938 (15-1)—Johnny Allen, Cleveland, 1937
 .889 (16-2)—Freddie Fitzimmons, Brooklyn, 1940

Most years leading league, percentage
 5—Bob (Lefty) Grove

Most no-hit games, lifetime
 4—Sandy Koufax

Fewest hits allowed, two consecutive games
 0—Johnny Vander Meer, Cincinnati, 1938

Most consecutive hitless innings, season
 23—Cy Young, Boston, AL, 1904

Most consecutive hitless innings, game
 12⅓—Harvey Haddix, Pittsburgh; Pittsburgh vs. Milwaukee, 1959

Most one-hit games, lifetime
 12—Bob Feller

Most shutout games, lifetime
 113—Walter Johnson
 90—Grover Alexander
 77—Cy Young

Most shutout games, season
 16—Grover Alexander, Philadelphia, NL, 1916
 13—John Coombs, Philadelphia, AL, 1910
 13—Bob Gibson, St. Louis, 1968

Most consecutive shutout games
 6—Don Drysdale, Los Angeles, 1968

Most consecutive shutout innings, game
 21—Joe Oeschger, Boston, NL; Boston vs. Brooklyn, 1920

Most consecutive shutout innings
 58—Don Drysdale, Los Angeles, 1968

Most strikeouts, lifetime
 3,497—Walter Johnson
 2,803—Cy Young
 2,583—Warren Spahn

Most strikeouts, season
382—Sandy Koufax, Los Angeles, 1965
349—Rube Waddell, Philadelphia, AL, 1904
348—Bob Feller, Cleveland, 1946

Most years leading league, strikeouts
12—Walter Johnson

Most years 300 or more strikeouts
3—Sandy Koufax

Most years 200 or more strikeouts
8—Bob Gibson

Most strikeouts, day game
19—Tom Seaver, New York, NL; New York vs. San Diego, 1970

Most strikeouts, night game
19—Steve Carlton, St. Louis; St. Louis vs. New York, NL, 1969

Most consecutive strikeouts
10—Tom Seaver, New York, NL; New York vs. San Diego, 1970

INDEX

Aaron, Hank, 54, 104
Abernathy, Ted, 29, 31
Acosta, Lou, 87
Adcock, Joe, 104
Agee, Tommy, 66
Alexander, Grover Cleveland, 116
All Star games, 23, 114
Allen, Richie, 47
American Association, 15
American League, 10, 17, 56, 70, 82, 92, 93, 111, 113, 114
Amoros, Sandy, 102
Arcia, Jose, 106
Arrigo, Gerry, 82
Atlanta Braves, 47, 48, 79

Babe Ruth Leagues, 22, 23
Baker, J. Franklin, 17
Baltimore Orioles, 44, 48, 62, 66, 113
Banks, Ernie, 47, 66
Barton, Bob, 105
Belanger, Mark, 66
Bench, Johnny, 60, 61, 79, 80, 82
Berra, Yogi, 102, 103
Blair, Paul, 62, 63, 66
Blue, Vida, 95
Boeckel, Tony, 96
Boston Braves, 96, 111
Boston Red Sox, 17, 32, 43, 74, 90, 98, 111, 113
Boston Red Stockings, 14, 16
Bouton, Jim, 66
Braves Field, 96
Briggs, Dr. Lyman, 56
Brooklyn Dodgers, 51, 96, 98, 99, 101
Brown, Professor F. N. M., 57

Bunning, Jim, 100
Burdette, Lew, 104

Cadore, Leon, 96, 97
California Angels, 26, 73, 83
Camilli, Dolph, 99
Campanella, Roy, 82, 102
Carlton, Steve, 105
Cartwright, Alexander, 12, 13
Catchers, 77-82
Catchers' signals, 77, 78, 79
Cepeda, Orlando, 54
Chadwick, Henry, 14, 15
Chance, Dean, 51
Chicago Cubs, 48, 51, 65, 115
Chicago White Sox, 70
Cincinnati Buckeyes, 13
Cincinnati Red Stockings, 13, 14
Cincinnati Reds, 42, 60, 76, 79, 80, 82
Clarke, Horace, 34
Clemente, Roberto, 20, 66
Cleveland Indians, 36, 108, 111
Cobb, Ty, 107, 110
Cochrane, Mickey, 82
Conigliaro, Tony, 66
Control, 60-61
Coombs, Dan, 31
Cooperstown, New York, 11, 12
Corkins, Mike, 105
Craft, Harry, 100
Creighton University, 9
Cronin, Joe, 114
Cruise, Wally, 96
Cuellar, Mike, 48, 49
Cummings, William Arthur (Candy), 39

Dean, Dizzy, 116
Delivery, 29-35, 61
Denver Bears, 27
Detroit Tigers, 10, 11, 27
Dickey, Bill, 82
Dierker, Larry, 89
Doubleday, Abner, 11, 14
Doubleday Field, 12
Dressen, Charlie, 77, 78
Drysdale, Don, 10, 64, 65
Durocher, Leo, 99, 100

Earned run average (ERA), 10, 51, 74, 75, 93, 109, 113, 115
Eastern League, 44
Ebbets Field, 98, 101
Elliot, Rody, 96
Ellis, Dock, 21
Elysian Fields, 13, 14
Etchebarren, Andy, 44

Feller, Bob, 36, 47, 56, 116
Ferrara, Al, 105, 106
Flick, Elmer, 17
Ford, Whitey, 43, 101, 115
Foxx, Jimmy, 114
Frisella, Danny, 49
Furillo, Carl, 102

Galvin, Jim, 15
Gaston, Clarence, 106
Gehrig, Lou, 114
Gehringer, Charlie, 114
Gibson, Bob, 9, 10, 11, 14, 19, 20, 36, 78
Giusti, Dave, 53, 71, 76

Gowdy, Hank, 96
Granger, Wayne, 76
Grant, Jim, 88
Grimes, Burleigh, 99
Grip, 37, 38, 42, 48
Grote, Jerry, 79
Grove, Robert (Lefty), 98, 108, 113, 115, 116

Haddix, Harvey, 103, 104
Hall of Fame and Museum, 12, 17, 98, 111
Hands, Bill, 65
Harrelson, Bud, 20
Hendricks, Elrod, 66
Hoak, Don, 104
Hodges, Gil, 102, 105
Holke, Walter, 96
Home plate, 14, 61, 80
Houston Astros, 89, 97, 98
Hubbell, Carl, 108, 113, 114, 115, 116
Hunter, Jim, 101

International League, 113

Johnson, Len, 97, 98
Johnson, Walter, 10, 107, 108, 113, 115, 116
Joss, Adrian, 100

Kansas City Royals, 29, 31
Kealey, Steve, 83
Keefe, Timothy, 16
Killebrew, Harmon, 67, 70
Knickerbockers, 12, 14
Koosman, Jerry, 40, 45, 58, 64
Koufax, Sandy, 36, 56, 57, 67, 98, 100, 108, 115
Koy, Ernie, 99

Kralick, John, 97
Krueger, Ernie, 96
Kucks, Johnny, 101
Kuhn, Commissioner Bowie, 20

Larsen, Don, 101, 102, 103
Lavagetto, Cookie, 99
Little Leagues, 9, 22, 23
Little Red Book of Baseball, The, 97, 101
Logan, Johnny, 104
Lolich, Mickey, 23, 27
Lombardi, Ernie, 99
Los Angeles Dodgers, 23, 47, 51, 64, 65, 82, 102
Lyle, Sparky, 90

Maglie, Sal, 102
Magnus, Professor G., 55
"Magnus effect," 55
Major leagues, 18, 27, 28
Maloney, Jim, 79, 81, 98
Mantilla, Felix, 104
Mantle, Mickey, 102
Manush, Heine, 114
Marichal, Juan, 10, 29, 45, 54
Mathewson, Christy, 108, 109, 110, 115, 116
Matthews, Ed, 104
Mays, Willie, 9
McCarver, Tim, 67
McDaniel, Lindy, 29, 49, 50, 74
McDowell, Sam, 70
McGraw, John, 109
McGraw, Tug, 61, 73
McKechnie, Bill, 98, 99
McNally, Dave, 23, 44, 45
Merritt, Jim, 43, 60, 61
Messersmith, Andy, 29, 44, 73

Milan, Clyde, 108
Milwaukee Braves, 103, 104
Minnesota Twins, 25, 70, 76, 97
Minor leagues, 27, 28
Mitchell, Dale, 102, 103
Montreal Expos, 91
Morehead, Dave, 98
Murrell, Ivan, 106
Murtaugh, Danny, 71

National Association of Professional Baseball Leagues, 14, 27
National League, 10, 14, 15, 16, 20, 47, 54, 56, 64, 66, 92, 93, 109, 113, 115
New York Giants, 16, 45, 48, 109, 110, 113
New York Metropolitans, 15
New York Mets, 20, 21, 30, 36, 40, 45, 51, 73, 79, 84, 89, 97, 105, 106
New York Yankees, 17, 23, 37, 43, 50, 62, 70, 83, 101
Newton, Sir Isaac, 30
Niekro, Phil, 47
Nolan, Gary, 42, 43

Oeschger, Joe, 96, 97
Old Timers' Day, 112
Olsen, Ivy, 96, 97

Palmer, Jim, 23, 93
Perranoski, Ron, 76
Perry, Gaylord, 51, 52
Peters, Gary, 32, 70
Peterson, Fritz, 23, 62, 63
Phelps, Babe, 99
Philadelphia Athletics, 14, 113
Philadelphia Phillies, 20, 21, 47, 104
Phillips, Lefty, 73

Pignatano, Joe, 84
Pitcher qualifications, 18, 19, 20, 21, 22, 23, 27, 28, 30, 32, 62
Pitchers' mound, 10, 11
Pitches, types, 14, 17, 18, 19, 20, 23, 29, 30, 35-45, 46-54, 60, 61
Pitching chart, 67, 69
Pitching coach, 83-85
Pitching strategy, 62-65
Pittsburgh Pirates, 21, 71, 87, 88, 89, 103, 104, 114
Powell, Boog, 63, 66
Providence, 14, 15

Radbourn, Charles, 14, 15, 116
Rayleigh, Lord John, 55
Record books, 97, 103, 108
Regan, Phil, 51
Reichardt, Rick, 25
Relief pitching, 71-76
Riggs, Lew, 99
Roberts, Dave, 62
Roberts, Robin, 20, 21
Robertson, Charles, 100
Robinson, Brooks, 66
Robinson, Frank, 66
Roe, Elwin (Preacher), 51
Rosen, Goody, 99
Rules, 12, 13, 14, 16, 17, 18, 51, 52
Rusie, Amos, 112
Ruth, Babe, 17, 114
Ryan, Nolan, 36, 37, 61

Sadecki, Ray, 30
St. Louis Browns, 101
St. Louis Cardinals, 9, 19, 26, 47, 104, 105, 111, 114
San Diego Padres, 31, 105
San Francisco Atlantics, 13
San Francisco Giants, 10, 51, 54
Santo, Ron, 65
Schofield, Dick, 104
Scouts, 23, 26
Seaver, Tom, 20, 21, 23, 61, 65, 79, 83, 90, 105, 106
Shamsky, Art, 80
Shaw, Bob, 51
Shea Stadium, 58, 89, 105
Sherry, Norm, 83
Shore, Ernie, 100
Sikorsky, Igor, 55, 56
Simmons, Al, 114
Singer, Bill, 64, 65
Spahn, Warren, 35, 38
Spaulding, A. G., 16, 55
Specialty pitches, 46-54
Spink, J. G. Taylor, 36
Sport Magazine, 20, 54
Sporting News, The, 36, 76, 92, 97
Stallings, George, 97
Standard pitches, 36-45
Stargell, Willie, 88
Statistics, 92-95
Stengel, Casey, 101, 102, 107
Stottlemyre, Mel, 23, 37, 63, 70
Strike zone, 10, 61

Swoboda, Ron, 62

Tatum, Ken, 34
Tillman, Bob, 79
Torre, Joe, 78
Training, 86-91
True, Denton, 110
Turner, Jim, 50, 83

Umpire, 14, 97, 103, 106

Vander Meer, Johnny, 98, 99, 100

Walker, Al (Rube), 45, 61, 83, 84, 105
Wallop, Douglass, 13
Washington Senators, 43, 107, 108
Webster, Ramon, 105
Wegener, Mike, 91
White, Will, 55
Wilhelm, Hoyt, 48
Williams, Ted, 43, 44
World Series, 14, 19, 51, 66, 101, 108, 109, 111, 113
Wright, Clyde, 98
Wright, George, 16
Wright, Harry, 14, 16

Yankee Stadium, 74, 102, 103
Yastrzemski, Carl, 10
Young, Cy, 100, 107, 108, 110, 111, 112, 113, 116

Zanger, Jack, 54

5